A Dove Under My Hand

A Dove Under My Hand

SAPPHIC WRITINGS BY MARINA TSVETAEVA

TRANSLATED BY SONJA FRANETA

A Sapphic Classic from
Sinister Wisdom

A Dove Under My Hand: Sapphic Writings by Marina Tsvetaeva
Translated by Sonja Franeta.

Editor and Publisher: Julie R. Enszer
Managing Editor: Shawn(ta) Smith-Cruz
Proofreader: Ellen Pearson
Cover and interior designed by Nieves Guerra.

Cover image from Vecteezy.com.
Cover media: many-birds-flying-on-sky-isolated-on-white-background from Vecteezy.com
Cover font: Squatina & Lexend
Back cover photo of Marina Tsvetaeva by Pierre Choumoff

Sinister Wisdom, Inc.
2333 McIntosh Road
Dover, FL 33527
sinisterwisdom@gmail.com
www.sinisterwisdom.org

First edition, September 2026
ISBN: 978-1-970841-02-2 print
ISBN: 978-1-970841-03-9 ebook
Library of Congress Cotrol Number: 2026942852

Printed in the U.S.
Price: $21.95

Two trees reach out to each other
The two trees. Across from my house.
They're old, the trees. My home is, too.
I'm young, otherwise I'd be
Going on about more trees.

The lesser one stretches out her limbs
Like a woman, to the limit,
Her veins straining—almost cruel
To watch how she stretches toward
The other one, the older one,
The one more stoic, yet more forlorn.

Two trees in the heat of the sunset
Beneath the rain, beneath the snow
Always, always—one to the other
The law of nature: one to the other
It's always so: one to another

Marina Tsvetaeva, 1919

Contents

Marina Tsvetaeva's Life

Marina Tsvetaeva was born October 9, 1892 in Moscow—her mother was a pianist and her father an art history professor. She began writing poetry at the age of six and produced her first book of poems in 1911 called *Evening Album.*

She met Sergey Efron, her future husband, in 1911 at a Crimean villa where writer Max Voloshin and his mother (who wore men's clothes) lived. She and Sergey married. She had her first daughter, Ariadna (also called Alya), in 1912. Tsvetaeva gave birth to her second child, Irina, the year of the Russian Revolution, 1917.

In 1914, Tsvetaeva and Sofia Parnok fell in love in Moscow; their love affair lasted two years until 1916. This was not her first attraction to a woman and it was not her last. She also had relationships with other men while married to Efron.

While working with a Studio of the Moscow Art Theater in 1919, Tsvetaeva met actress Sonia Holliday (Sonechka Gollidey) and others. In the years after the revolution, Tsvetaeva and her family faced extreme hardship; Tsvetaeva's younger child, Irina, died of starvation at a state-run boarding school. In spite of these challenges, Tsvetaeva published several books of poetry. In 1922, with her daughter, Ariadna, she emigrated to Europe, first to Berlin, then to Prague, joining her husband who had fled and was doing political work. Her son Georgy (called Mur) was born in 1925.

From 1925–1938, Tsvetaeva lived in Paris among the Russian emigre community During these years, she was impoverished and felt isolated. She wrote *Lettre à l'Amazone* (1932, revised in 1934) in French. In 1937, Tsvetaeva's daughter Ariadna went back to the Soviet Union, following her father who had become a double agent working with both pro-Soviet factions and opponents of the revolution. Tsvetaeva wrote *Story of Sonechka* looking back at her 1919 experiences in 1937. It was her last prose work. In 1939, Tsvetaeva decided to return to Moscow with her son to join her daughter and husband, but they were imprisoned soon after she arrived. In 1941, Tsvetaeva and her son were evacuated to remote Yelabuga because of World War II. Tsvetaeva ended her life there because, in her words, she "had come to a dead end." She was 48 when she died.

Tsvetaeva's husband was executed for espionage that same year, though she did not know about this at the time of her death. Their daughter Ariadna was arrested and tortured to betray her father then sent to the gulag for conspiracy. She spent sixteen years there. Ariadna was released when she was fifty-five years old. While in the gulag she met another woman prisoner, Ada Federolf, with whom she subsequently lived in Tarusa, near Moscow, when they were released. Their intimate relationship and mutual support helped them survive the brutal arctic Turukhansk gulag. After her release, Ariadna devoted herself to organizing and collecting her mother's work. Ariadna wrote several memoirs about her life and her mother's. She died in 1975.

With the turmoil and constant movement in war and revolution, it is extraordinary how much of Marina Tsvetaeva's work survived. An archive and library of her works is in Moscow at the Marina Tsvetaeva House Museum where she used to live, on Boris and Gleb Lane. Most of her works have been published in Russian as well as in translation in other languages.

Anastasia Tsvetaeva, Marina's sister, was also a writer and was sent to the gulag for "counter-revolutionary activities." She was released in 1959 after twenty-two years of imprisonment. Archival collections of both Marina and Anastasia are at the University of Kentucky in Lexington.

Introduction

One of the most chaotic and terrifying periods in Russian history was the post-Revolution civil war which extended from 1917 until 1923. People were starving, living without comforts or necessities, worried about violence and theft, surrounded by death and disease. There was extreme insecurity and devastation. In 1937, Marina Tsvetaeva [pronounced SVE-**TA**-YE-VA] remembers her life in 1919, when she was involved in a theater world with a queer cadence, and writes *Story of Sonechka.* This poetic novella is her last prose work. The *Story of Sonechka* captures Tsvetaeva's love for Sonechka as well as the gay men she knew at the time—Pavel and Yura and Volodya. The theater world was an escape from the very male, violent maelstrom in the years following the revolution. In *Story of Sonechka*, Tsvetaeva focuses on her love for Sonechka Holliday (Gollidey in Russian), a child-like actress, and portrays her through stream-of-consciousness monologues as a frivolous, self-centered, feminine actress. Tsvetaeva writes about Sonechka, "She was a female being whom I loved more than anyone else in the world. Perhaps more than all beings, male or female."

Tsvetaeva confides, "It was difficult to even speak of her as a 'friend,' she was simply 'Love' in its feminine form in my life; I have never loved someone so much." In the *Story of Sonechka*, Tsvetaeva grapples with the connections between performance and gender and love. Tsvetaeva creates a new kind of eroticism, a love and appreciation for women, a fluidity of sexual desire beyond the physical, and a questioning of sexual identity and gender roles.

When Sonechka leaves her, Tsvetaeva makes a profound statement about the banality of heteronormativity:

"Sonechka abandoned me—and went to her feminine destiny. Not coming back was her way of complying with her feminine destiny: to love a man—in the end, it didn't matter which man—and to love him alone until the end."

Then she wryly observes, "The two of us went against 'society,' that's all: but never against God and never against man."

In the early part of the twentieth century, many artists and writers lived in non-traditional relationships including same-gendered partnerships. Although Tsvetaeva always felt different, she married the eighteen-year-old Sergey Efron in 1912, when she was nineteen. Prior to her marriage, she had been in love with girls. In early poems she wrote "I love women who knew no fear in battle," yet in the same poem she speaks of how she and her sisters are destined for the prison of "rocking a cradle." Although she loved her children and husband, she dared to be different and have other loves throughout her life. Was Tsvetaeva bisexual or lesbian? With contemporary language, Tsvetaeva may have identified as queer. How she viewed her sexuality is unknown but her work is compelling to contemporary lesbian and queer women readers.

Before the Russian Revolution and during the very bohemian Silver Age of Russian literature, Tsvetaeva was only twenty-two. She met the eccentric Sofia Parnok, who was seven years older, at a salon in Moscow. Tsvetaeva was instantly attracted to her: Parnok's high forehead and fine eyebrows and direct look. Tsvetaeva liked people who were different but her attraction to Parnok was far more powerful. She wrote in one of the *Girlfriend Poems,* "Not a woman, not a boy/something stronger than me." Calling this woman Orestes, with a mix of male and female imagery, she likely knew Parnok was openly lesbian! Everyone knew. Tsvetaeva wanted her. She was unafraid. She wrote, "Love me, oh love me!" Imagine what she said to Parnok.

As a couple, they were embraced by their circles of friends and artists. Salons in Moscow and St. Petersburg were popular gathering places for poets, artists, musicians. They also traveled to the Crimea together, a popular Russian holiday destination on the Black Sea. Even though Tsvetaeva was married to Efron and had a small child, Ariadna, she socialized boldly in the literary world, accompanied by Parnok for almost two years. In Russia at the time, free love and same-sex love were popularly accepted, especially among bohemian artistic circles. Parnok's legendary affairs with women were no secret.

In January 1916, Tsvetaeva and Parnok went to St. Petersburg to visit gay poet Mikhail Kuzmin's new salon. In St. Petersburg, Tsvetaeva met with her friend the poet Osip Mandelstam on several occasions. Parnok became jealous of Mandelstam, and Tsvetaeva and Parnok had several quarrels about him. When it came time to go to Kuzmin's salon, Parnok complained of a headache. Tsvetaeva went on her own. When she returned, Parnok was flirting with another woman. While we don't know the reasons for their breakup—there were conflicts—this flirtation seemed like the final straw.

Tsvetaeva called this moment the first catastrophe of her life. After all their emotions, arguments, and confessions of love! After all the poems! Tsvetaeva relegated her love affair to "a mistake." It was a deceit of the highest order, a betrayal! One story suggests she even asked Sofia for her copy of the *Girlfriend Poems* and then shoved them away somewhere, never allowing them to see the light of day or be published in her lifetime.

Yet Tsvetaeva's love poems for Parnok survived. These poems are the earliest expression of eroticism and sexual desire in same-sex love in Russian literature. While Tsvetaeva and Parnok parted in turmoil and Tsvetaeva was deeply hurt, the memory of this relationship pursued her for the rest of her life, no matter how much she tried to forget.

The *Girlfriend Poems* have a lightness and heart of youth. While Parnok was not the first or last woman Tsvetaeva loved, she was the only open lesbian that Tsvetaeva fell in love with, and it was perhaps her most intense physical relationship.

Tsvetaeva emigrated with her daughter after the devastating famine during War Communism (the period right after the revolution) and eventually joined her husband. She left Russia in 1922, going first to Berlin then Prague and finally Paris, encountering other romantic infatuations for both women and men. In 1931, Marina Tsvetaeva wrote a friend about "her great longing for a loving relationship with a woman." In 1932, another friend of Tsvetaeva's brought her to meet the famous lesbian Natalie Barney in Paris. It was a brief meeting, and the wealthy socialite Barney was surely not impressed with the frumpy, poorly dressed, unknown Russian poet. About a month later Tsvetaeva started writing *Letter to an Amazon* in reply to Natalie Barney and her book *Pensees d'une Amazone* (1920).

Letter to an Amazon is Tsvetaeva's final good-bye to Sofia Parnok, her first woman lover. Parnok died in August of 1933, between the two known versions of the *Letter.* It is clear Tsvetaeva lived with her love and feeling of betrayal by her Amazon all her life. She writes:

"And so what, if she has died? After all I, too, will die someday . . . With courage and with the highest honesty and indifference, I say—

"Hasn't she has died within me, and for me—already twenty years ago?"

In *Letter to an Amazon,* Tsvetaeva portrays two women, one older and one younger, who have chosen a life together. They are happy with each other, until the day the younger one is struck by her maternal instinct. Then she is more interested in having a child than a same-sex relationship, but she does not necessarily want to be with a man either. The tone is mournful—about a relationship between women unable to sustain itself.

Today, of course, lesbians can and do create families, but the ongoing problems under patriarchy for lesbians are far from solved. Despite her belief in the maternal instinct, Tsvetaeva was drawn to Barney's salon and to lesbian relationships because, for her, love went beyond gender lines. Themes of Amazons, Sappho, and her unrequited loves, like the one with her benefactor Salomea Halpern (see her letter to Salomea at the end of this book), all nurtured Tsvetaeva's life of passion.

The State repressions during the Soviet period (1922-1991) were enormous. Prohibitions against lyrical poetry were responsible for the obscurity of Marina Tsvetaeva's poetry as well as Sofia Parnok's. Great writers and artists, who Tsvetaeva admired, had already been killed or killed themselves because of Stalin's fierce repression including Vladimir Mayakovsky, Sergey Esenin, Osip Mandelstam. Lyric poetry was forbidden by law; most poets wrote for themselves or for a small circle. Boris Pasternak's great novel *Doctor Zhivago* was smuggled to Milan in 1957 to be published. He won the Nobel Prize for it but was not allowed to accept it. Anna Akhmatova memorized her own poems to pass them on. She even memorized some of Tsevateva's and those of other poets to give them life and a future.

The Soviet Union was not proud of one of its greatest twentieth-century poets. Even though Marina Tsvetaeva was a respected poet during her life, it was not until the 1970s and 1980s that her work became accessible to people in the Soviet Union, mainly through the work of her daughter Ariadna. In Leningrad (St. Petersburg's Soviet name), lesbian scholar Sofia Polyakova combed bookstores and found manuscripts by Tsvetaeva and Parnok. She explored the relationship between these two poets at the end of the 1970s in her book, *The Sunset Days of*

Yore: Tsvetaeva and Parnok. The book is only available in Russian but was smuggled into the US and published by Ardis Press in Michigan. In this radical lesbian book, Polyakova published the entire *Girlfriend* [Podruga, in Russian] cycle of poems along with a commentary about the women's lives and relationship, revealing Marina and Sofia's sapphic relationship to the world. After this, Marina Tsvetaeva became a lesbian and queer icon.

Creating this book of translations of work by Marina Tsvetaeva has been a lifelong dream. Ever since I was in college at NYU—studying Russian and discovering Russian literature—I was captivated by Tsvetaeva's poetry. I wanted to get better at Russian just to read Tsvetaeva and other Russian writers. My first language was Serbo-Croatian, the language of my parents who had emigrated to the US after the ravages of World War II in Europe. They were from the former Yugoslavia. I was drawn to the Russian language because of its closeness to Serbo-Croatian. I found such a literary abundance in the Russian writers, and I never lost interest. At the university I became fascinated by the craft of translating—finding the right word, matching the writer's style, and concentrating on making the work of art luminous. I continued to develop these skills while nurturing my own writing.

Tsvetaeva was one of my mentors in writing. Tsvetaeva's poetry inspired me with its rhythms, its rhymes, its words and ideas, and she continues to inspire me with her prose. Translating her work brought me greater appreciation for it. One cannot replicate a poem from one language to another. It is recreated and becomes a new piece of literature. When I translated anything by Tsvetaeva, for example, I would look at her poem, with a deep understanding of her context and her life, and, as closely as I could, I would reflect on what I thought she wanted to say. Then I would edit and produce a translation. Literary translating is a creative act and a dance that one does with another artist.

The pieces in this collection are Tsvetaeva's major lesbian writings. *Story of Sonechka* is about Marina Tsvetaeva's love for a woman and her refuge in the theater during turmoil of revolution and devastation. Tsvetaeva, in a kind of stream of consciousness, captures the speech of this butterfly of a woman and helps us visualize Sonechka as if she is doing a solo show. For Tsvetaeva, Sonechka turns out to be an otherworldly love—a love that holds all the love she has felt over the years. This autobiographical memoir with fragments, scenes, poetry, and dialogue shows a woman, a poet, struggling with the insecurities of the times and in her personal life. Her poetic and fragmentary style invites readers into a most unusual world.

The *Girlfriend Poems* are a clear and delightful early expression of same-sex love. Tsvetaeva wrote them during her affair with Sofia Parnok and they beautifully portray the eroticism and romance between the two lovers.

Letter to an Amazon is addressed to Natalie Barney. The essay explores the beauty of lesbian love and its ultimate impossibility, at least for Tsvetaeva.

Ending this book is an intense letter Tsvetaeva wrote to Salomea Halpern around the same time she finished *Letter to an Amazon*. In order to survive as a writer, Tsvetaeva had several women benefactors. One of them was Salomea Halpern, formerly a Georgian princess. She gave Tsvetaeva a third of her monthly salary from 1926 to 1934. Marina and Salomea had an extensive letter exchange over the years. In this letter, Tsvetaeva wrote to Salomea, "I loved you with such fervor (a silent frenzy), I wanted you to the point of self-annihilation . . ."

The four works in this translation are connected. When Sofia Parnok died in 1933 surrounded by her women's community, she had a photo of Tsvetaeva at her bedside. At the very same time, Tsvetaeva was still battling the demons of Sofia Parnok's betrayal. While writing *Letter to an Amazon*, rationalizing her beautiful and stormy relationship, she was referring to the loss of her past love, Parnok. In *Letter to an Amazon*, it wasn't a man the younger lover was after but a child. Was Tsvetaeva the younger lover in question—the one who yearned for children? Though Sofia Parnok was seven years older than Tsvetaeva, they ironically died at the same age. Parnok died of heart disease at forty-eight. Tsvetaeva, too, was forty-eight when she took her life.

Tsvetaeva dared to be different and loved those who were different. She loved the great poet Osip Mandelstam who was imprisoned and died in the gulag for a negative comment about Stalin. Nadezhda, his wife, wrote this about Tsvetaeva: "My impression of Tsvetaeva was that she was absolutely natural and fantastically self-willed. I have a vivid recollection of her cropped hair, loose-limbed gait like a boy's—and speech remarkably like her verse."

The many sides of Tsvetaeva—bisexual, lesbian, nonbinary, queer, androgynous, genderqueer—were not named in the times she lived. Tsvetaeva came closest to naming with the image of the Amazon. She wrote this poem in 1921:

Woman's breast! Stark sigh of the soul—
Woman's essence! A wave of surprise,
Caught off guard—always catching
One unawares—but God sees!

Plaything of pleasures scorned
And despised—a woman's breast!
Armor yielding—I'm thinking of those . . .
Single-breasted ones—those girlfriends! . . .

In the summer of 1977, I had been married to a man for six years, but I had been dreaming about women. In Moscow, traveling with a group of UK socialists, I fell in love with an American woman in the group. It was my first relationship with a woman. I had not yet joined the women's liberation movement even from afar, but it awakened in me an interest in lesbian relationships. In California, where I was living, it felt like a wonderful blossoming time for women—with a strong Sapphic touch. It was a time of identity and commitment in the face of a heteronormative, patriarchal world, but in Moscow, I was coming out in one of the most repressive countries in the world.

I still remember when she and I were in a woodsy area called Lenin Hills (later renamed to its previous Sparrow Hills) overlooking the Moscow River, with expansive views of the city. Feeling safe and somewhat hidden by the full green trees, we kissed. It was as delicious as it was dangerous. Tsvetaeva and many other writers and artists had found inspiration here. Later I learned it was even a famous meeting place for queers of all kinds, especially in the evenings—there in the woods, high above the river.

I had known already about Tsvetaeva's poetry in this, my transformational year. After I came out, imagine my excitement and affinity when I learned about Tsvetaeva's strong interest in women and her love affair with a woman at the age of twenty-two, while she was still married and had a child.

In the 1990s, when I met lesbians during my travels through the former Soviet Union, many of them spoke proudly about Tsvetaeva and Parnok as their heroes and gave me Marina's books as presents. If in the past they thought they were "the only ones," now they knew that not only their greatest composer Tchaikovsky was queer but one of their greatest poets Marina Tsvetaeva was, too. Like me, they were learning about this legacy for the first time

Perestroika was a time of big changes in the Soviet Union. In July of 1991, I was honored to be part of the first North American queer delegation to the Soviet Union. It was their first Gay and Lesbian Symposium and Film Festival. Initially, there was some shyness, but after a while with the help of translators, people got to know one another and relationships and liaisons were formed. We had conferences in Leningrad (St. Petersburg) and Moscow and then a film festival in Moscow attended by thousands. It was truly a wonderful time—another life-changing moment for me, fourteen years after my coming out trip in 1977.

After decades of having to be secretive and being cut off from any influences and media outside of the Soviet Union, people who felt they were sexual minorities (as they were called) were able to be themselves openly. During the 1990s, the changes that took place there were extraordinary. The law (Article 121) that made gay sexual relations illegal was repealed, the media began to print articles, and TV featured interviews about LGBTQ people. Organizations and journals and magazines were initiated—a queer internet site called gay.ru was launched.

During those years, I interviewed many LGBTQ people who had never talked explicitly about their lives as lesbian, gay, bi, or trans. I am so grateful for their candor and trust. With the help of friends at the Moscow LGBT Archives, my book of interviews called *Pink Flamingos: 10 Siberian Interviews* was published in Russian (in 2004). It was sold out that same year. In 1999, a lesbian quarterly called *Ostrov* (Island) was launched in Moscow and its editor, Olgerta Kharitonova, has written an afterward for this book. She reflects the ideas of many lesbians of the time. The overall opinion in Russia was still prejudiced and homophobic but more and more queers felt comfortable coming out. In St. Petersburg, in Tomsk Siberia, and in other cities, film festivals and other queer events took place. An LGBT Archive was started in Moscow. Now, all of this has been repressed by Putin and his oligarchy, and many queers have emigrated. Queer books and publications are banned, some activists are in prison, and any signs or even words alluding to the idea of queer are forbidden, including of course, rainbows.

Tsvetaeva's life was all about poetry and love. Her loves were many, no matter the gender. Tsvetaeva gives us the wisdom and courage—still as relevant and queer and passionate as when she wrote—we would go into whatever hell we have ahead.

I wonder what Tsvetaeva would have thought about today's Russia. Reading Tsvetaeva's work she seems to predict the demise of the world and of love. As far back as 1915, during her time with Sofia Parnok, she wrote:

"We are sure to end up in hell / oh my ardent sisters."

Story of Sonechka: A Woman's Life

Part One
Pavlik and Yuri

Pale, pale—and yet pink
Petite—but with the grandest hair . . .

No, there was not one bit of paleness about her, not one bit, everything about her was really just the opposite of pale, yet she was indeed "pourtant rose," and that will be discussed and proven in time.

It was winter of 1918-1919—no, not quite winter, December of 1918. I was performing at some theater, on some stage, my play, *Blizzard,* before the students of Studio Three. To an empty theater, on a full stage.

My *Blizzard* was dedicated to "Yuri and Vera Z., their friendship, my love." Yuri and Vera were brother and sister, Vera was a fellow student at the last high school I attended, not a classmate because I was a year ahead. I used to see her at class changes: a thin, curly-headed, girlish puppy dog. I especially remember her long back with her partly-undone braid. But it was her mouth—a grimace with corners turned down, and her eyes did the opposite of her mouth, they smiled, corners upturned. This divergence of lines produced in me an inexplicable feeling of agitation, which I translated as her beauty; this, in turn, surprised everyone else who found nothing of the sort in her, which bothered me immensely. Here I'd like to say I was right—she turned into such a beauty, truly, that in 1927 in Paris, when she was seriously ill, even with her last ounce of energy, they managed to drag her onto the stage.

This Vera . . . I never said a word to her, this Vera . . . now, nine years later, after dedicating *Blizzard* to her . . . now, thinking with trepidation that she would not understand at all, because she surely did not remember me and perhaps never even noticed me.

(But why Vera, when there was Sonechka? Vera is the root, the prehistory, the very inception of Sonechka. It's a very short story—with a very long prehistory. And a post-history.)

How did Sonechka begin? For me, she began full of life.

It was October of 1917. Yes, that one. The very last day of October, that is, the first day after the end (we were still dodging behind barricades). I was riding in a dark train compartment from Moscow to the Crimea. Above my head, from an upper berth, a young male voice was going on and on poetically. This is what he recited:

Here she is, the old men dreamed of her
And noisily argued over cognac,
Cloak of Gironde, through snow and woe
They came toward us—with pointed bayonets!

And ghosts of Decembrist guardsmen
Over the snowy Neva, Pushkin's Neva,
Came like regiments at the call of a horn,
With the loud howl of military music.

The Emperor himself in bronze boots
Called you, the Preobrazhensky's Regiment,
When in the stream of prostrate streets
A jaunty clarinet broke into sound and fell silent. . . .

And remembered the Miracle Builder,
Attentive to the Peter and Paul gunfire—

That crazy—strange—rebellious one
That memorable voice: You![I]

"What is that, who wrote that?"

"The author is only seventeen, he is still in high school. It's my friend Pavlik."

The cadet was proud to have a friend who was a poet. A combat junker, five days out of combat. Getting even with defeat through poetry. Fragrance of Pushkin: themes of friendship. And from above, a retort:

"He's very much like Pushkin. Short, nimble, curly-headed, sideburns, even the boys in Pushkin [the city] called him Pushkin. Always writing. Every morning a new poem.

Infanta [Little Princess], know that I am ready to go to any bonfire

If I knew your eyes were looking at me,

Your eyes . . .

"And isn't that from *Infanta's Doll*, his play? A dwarf is speaking to Infanta. The dwarf loved the Infanta Princess. The dwarf. He's very small, but not exactly a dwarf.

The only one—with many names . . .

***

The very first thing I did when I returned from the Crimea was to look for Pavlik. Pavlik lived somewhere near the Cathedral of Christ the Savior and for some reason I arrived at his back door and we got together in his kitchen. Pavlik was in his high school uniform, with those buttons that further emphasized his similarity to the lycee-attending Pushkin. Little Pushkin, only with dark eyes: the legendary Pushkin.

Neither he nor I were ashamed of being in the kitchen, we were smushed together by the pots and pans—so that we clattered within—like the pots and pans. Our meeting was like an earthquake. Just as I figured out who he was, he figured out who I was. (I am not even talking about poetry. I don't even know if he knew my poetry then.)

I don't know how long we stood still in a magical stupor. Suddenly we both walked out the same back door, bursting with lines of poetry . . .

In short, Pavlik just disappeared. He abandoned me on Boris and Gleb Lane for a very long time. For days, mornings, nights, we would sit still . . . I could give an example of this stillness, with one exchange.

I'd say timidly: "Pavlik, what do you think? Can we call what we are now doing—thinking?"

Pavlik, even more timidly: "It's called sitting in the clouds and ruling the world."

***

Pavlik had a friend, Yuri Z. [Yura], who he always talked about: "Yuri and I . . . I read this to Yuri . . . You know . . . Yuri was always asking me . . . Yesterday Yura and I kissed each other loudly on purpose, so people would think Yura and I finally fell in love . . . and believe it or not: studio members rushed in to see and instead of a girl—they saw it was me!"

And one fine evening he brought me this "Yura."

"Now this is Marina. And this is my friend—Yura Z., he said with the same weight and stress on each word."

Gazing upward, which took a lot of time, because Yuri wasn't finished growing, I started seeing Vera's eyes and mouth!

"Lord, are you the brother . . . Yes, of course, you're her brother . . . But you can't be Vera's brother!"

"He loves her more than anything in the world!"

We started to talk, Yura and I. Yura and I talked, while Pavlik was silent and silently devoured us, together and apart, with his huge deep dark eyes.

That same evening, that night, was intense, then in the early morning we parted under the poplars. I wrote them a poem, for the two of them together:

They sleep, not separating their hands
Brother to brother, friend to friend
Together on one bed
Together they drink, together they sing . . .

I wrapped them in a small blanket
I forever fell in love with them
I, through closed lids
Read the strangest news:
Rainbow: double glory
Fire: double death.

I can't part these hands!
I'll be better, better I'll be,
Let's all burn in hell!

But instead of "burn" it came out as—*Blizzard.*

In order to keep my word and not separate *their* hands, I had to intertwine other hands for me to love: a brother's and sister's. To put it simply: I could not love *just* Yura alone and thereby drive away Pavlik, with whom I had to "jointly rule the world." I had to love Yura plus something else, but that something could not be Pavlik, because Yura plus Pavlik were already a given. I had to love Yura plus Vera, to distract Yuri, but in fact it was a strengthening, a concentration; whatever was not in the brother, we found in the sister and all that was not in the sister we found in the brother. Bestowed on me was this terribly full, unbearably full love. (Vera, ailing in the Crimea, had no idea of any of it. And it didn't change anything.)

The relationship was determined—from the very beginning.

It was tacitly agreed upon and understood, they would always come over together and leave together. But, since no relationship could be fixed like that from the start, one fine morning the telephone rang:

"Is it you?"

"Yes, it's me."

"Could I come over sometime without Pavlik?"

"When?"

"Today."

(So where was Sonechka? Sonechka was really quite close, almost at the door, although in real time—a year away.)

But the crime was punished then and there: Yura Z. and me, when we were by ourselves, were bored, I mean both of us were, him and me, me and him, we didn't dare talk (we were even more restrained by ourselves than when we were with Pavlik!), all the rest was a big failure. He kept touching little things on my table and asking me about my photographs, and I couldn't even talk to him about Vera. Before this, Vera was—him. So we'd sit, not knowing what we were waiting for, waiting for a one-minute goodbye, while I escorted him to the back door and down the wooden stairs, stopping on the last step. At any rate he still ended up being a head taller—only at a glance—yes, no, maybe so?—and then again—is it—that *double*-edged smile—to his great amazement, I worked up some enthusiasm. (One more triumph like this and we are done for.)

That's how the year went.

I didn't read my *Blizzard* to him that January of 1918. Only a person with a very rich life could be satisfied with solitude, and during our long sessions he didn't seem like that kind of person. Yet Pavlik did seem very that way—so I presented it to Pavlik as an answer to his *Infanta*, which was not even dedicated to me. For Yuri—I waited and chose to read the most difficult part of the play (not at all gratifying for me), and in front of the entire Studio Three[II] (all Vakhtangov's proteges—Yuri, Pavlik, and the one in the dark railroad car who read "Liberty" and was subsequently killed in the war), and most importantly, in front of Vakhtangov who was their god and their father/commander.

After all, my goal was to bestow him with more and more—the actor in him—with more people around, more ears to hear, more eyes to see . . .

And here, more than a year later, after being introduced to this hero, an entire year after writing *Blizzard*—it was that very same full stage and no audience.

(My precision is annoying, I know. I'm sure the reader does not care about dates. It ruins the artistic quality of the work. For me, however, they are vital, even sacred, for me every year, each season of that time is connected to a face: 1917—to Pavlik A., Winter of 1918—to Yura Z., Spring of 1919—to Sonechka . . . I just don't see her beyond the number nine, the two ones and the two nines, alternating ones and nines . . . My precision is my final, posthumous fidelity.)

There was that very full stage and no audience. A bright stage and a dark theater.

From the first moment of my reading, my face flared, and since I was scared my hair lit up, I could even feel it lightly crackling, like right before a fire catches.

I recited—I could say—in a scarlet fog, not seeing my notebook, not seeing the lines before me, I recited from memory, at random, in one breath—in a sing-song voice—and oh how we sang!—the most melodious, singing from our hearts.

. . . And the high moon sails into deserted nobles' rooms.
You a woman, you hold back nothing.
You don't remember . . .
(insisting)

To the woman wanderer it is a dream.
To the male wanderer, a path.
Remember!—Forget.
(She sleeps. Outside the window, faraway bells chime with no return.)

When I finished reading—everyone started speaking at once. And they spoke up so *loudly* as soon as I fell silent. Magnificent! Extraordinary! Brilliant! Dramatic! and so on. "Yura will play the merchant" "And Lilia S. the old woman" "And Yura S. the merchant" "And the music will be those very bells with no return"—said Yura N. "But who will play the Woman in the Shawl?"

And the most shameful judgments right to my face: "You—of course not: you have a big bust." (Or: your legs are too short.)

(Quietly, I said: "The Woman in the Shawl is my soul. No one can play her.")

Everyone talked, and I was on fire. After they finished, they became overly appreciative. "An immersive pleasure . . . a singular delight . . ." All the faces, the strangers were useless. Finally—the Gentleman in the Shawl. He didn't come, he only walked away, using his height and his shawl to disconnect me from the others. He stood with me at the edge of the stage:

"Only Verochka can play the Woman in the Shawl. Only Verochka."

Their friendship—my love?

"And this, Marina," said Pavlik in a low, solemn voice, "is Sofia Evgenievna Gollidey" The same as just a year ago. "And,

Marina, this is my friend—Yura Z." Only, along with the words, *my friend*, there was a little swallow. (At that very moment, I felt something near my shoulder—Yura Z. had left.)

Before me was a small girl. *I knew it*, Pavlik's Infanta! With two dark braids, two large dark eyes, and two cheeks on fire.

Before me—a live fire. Lighting up everything, engulfing—her cheeks, her lips, her eyes, white teeth on fire in her mouth, burning and curling in a flame!—her two dark braids, one on her back, the other on her chest, as if one was cast aside by the fire. And the look from behind this fire was full of admiration, full of despair: I am afraid! And so: I love!

"Does this kind of thing really happen? Inns like this, blizzards, these love affairs . . . Gentlemen in shawls who arrive for a reason then leave forever? I always knew this—happened, now I know that this—exists. Because it truly occurred: you really stood there like that. Because it was *you* who stood there. The old woman sat down. She knew everything. And the blizzard raged. And the blizzard drove him to the threshold. And then afterwards he was swept back . . . covering her tracks . . . But what happened when she got up the next day? She never got up . . . They found her in a field . . . And why oh why didn't he take her with him in the sleigh? Why didn't he wrap her and take her away in his fur coat?"

Mumbling, as if in her sleep. Wide open eyes—she's asleep, really sleeping. As if she and I were all alone, and there was no one else, and really, not even me. And when I, with a sense of release, finally looked around, indeed there was no one onstage: everyone sensed it or, used the moment, to quietly, silently, leave. The stage was—ours.

It was at this point that I noticed I was still holding her little hand in my hand.

***

"Oh Marina! I got so scared! Then I cried . . . When I saw you the first time, heard you, right away I fell so madly in love with you, and I knew that a person could not help but madly fall in love with you. I myself fell so in love with you right away."

"And did he *not* love you?"

"No, and now it's over. I don't love him anymore. I love you. But him, I hate him for not loving you—prostrate before you and on his knees."

"Sonechka! Didn't you notice how my face was burning up?"

"Burning up? No. I even thought how soft and rosy . . ."

"So that means I must have been burning inside, and I was afraid the whole stage, the whole theater, the whole of Moscow would catch fire. I was thinking that it was because of him—for him—him and me—that I was reading for him—in front of everyone—for the first time. Now I know: that I was burning up because of meeting you, Sonechka . . . It wasn't me, nor you. It was love that took hold. Our love."

It was December of 1918. It was my final blush. All of Sonechka—my final blush. From about that time began that color—a non-color on my face, and a non-color that will most likely never leave me—until the very last colorlessness.

Was it flaring up seeing her? Or was it a reflection of her brief yet enduring flame?

. . . I am so happy that my final blush came with Sonechka.

***

"Sonechka, where did you come from—with your crazy life—you don't sleep, you don't eat, you cry, you love—and why this blush on your cheeks?"

"Oh Marina! It's with the last of my strength!"

***

And here the first part of my epigraph was confirmed:

Pale, pale—and yet pink[III]

She was pale—with all her pains—she should have been pale, but, really, after summoning up all her might—she was burning up. Sonechka's blush was the blush of a hero. A person who has decided to blaze and burn. I often saw her in the mornings, after one of my sleepless nights, in those early, early hours, after a late, late conversation, when all the faces—even the youngest—were that greenish color of sky in a window, the color of sunrise. But no! Sonechka's small dark-eyed face glowed, like an unextinguished pink street lamp in a harbor alley—yes, of course, it was a port, and she—the street lamp—and all the rest of us were that poor, poor sailor, who knew it was time to get back on the ship to mop the decks and take on a wave . . .

***

Sonechka, I am writing to you from the Ocean (Oh, if only it could sound like this: "the Ocean I am writing from" but no:)—I am writing to you on the Ocean, on which you have never been and never will be. At its edges, and mainly, on its islands, where many dark-eyed ones live. The sailors know.

***

She had a laugh close to tears and tears close to a laugh—I do not remember them running down her face. You could say that her eyes were too warm to let them run, for they dried as soon as they appeared. That was why those beautiful eyes, always ready to cry, were not moist . . . on the contrary—those eyes, while shiny with tears, gave off heat, gave the image, the sensation of warmth—and not moisture, since with all her good will—the bad will of others—she did not let a single one escape.

And yet—yes!

Beautiful, beautiful, like grapes, and I swear to you they were burning, and seeing her cry—one can laugh with pleasure! Is it possible they mean this when they say, "crying hot tears?" If so, I have seen a human with truly hot tears. All the others, mine, like those of the other people, are cold or lukewarm, but hers were burning, and the fire of her cheeks were so powerful you could see them falling—rose red. Hot like blood, round like pearls, salty like sea.

. . . It was like she was crying to Mozart.

***

This is how Edmond About pictures Sonechka's eyes in his marvelous book *The King of the Mountains*.[IV]

What eyes she had, my dear Sir! I wish that for your own peace of mind you will never find any like these. They were neither blue nor black, but a color particular to her and personally made for her. It was an ardent brown, a velvety color which you can only find in the Siberian garnet and in certain garden flowers. I will show you a scabiosa and a variety of hollyhock, almost black, that is reminiscent of, but not quite reaching, the nuance of her marvelous eyes. If you have ever visited the ironworks at midnight, you would have noticed the eerie reddish-brown glow projected by a hot steel plate: that is the color of her gaze. The entire wisdom of woman and all the innocence of a child you'd read, in her irises, as in a book . . . but this book, you would go blind reading too long. Her burning gaze, as true as my name is Hermann. It would make the peaches on your trellis ripen.

Was Pavlik's exclamation clear now?

Know that I am ready to go to any bonfire
If I knew your eyes were watching me—
Your eyes . . .

As for me, I was more modest:

Brown eyes, color of a chestnut horse, with a little gold deep inside, dark brown and amber—deep inside—not Baltic amber but reddish, Eastern amber. Almost black with a reddish gold deep inside, which at times surfaces: molten amber: eyes melting with molten amber—deep inside.

I also want to say: her eyes squinted a bit: so thick were her eyelashes that they could prevent her from seeing, but they didn't prevent us from seeing them, her eyes, like rays that can't prevent us from seeing a star. One more thing: even when she cried—her eyes smiled. That's why her tears weren't believable. Moscow doesn't believe in tears. The Moscow of that time didn't believe those tears. Only I believed in them.

She was not trusted, in general. Actually, even with my resounding enthusiasm far and wide, there were reservations . . . and these very reservations, out of respect for me, clearly were judgmental and condemning.

"Yes, she was very talented . . . But she was an actress with only one role: her own. I mean, she played herself and that means she didn't act at all. She—just lives. After all, that's Sonechka in her room, in her house—and it's the same Sonechka on stage . . ."

***

Sonechka on stage:

She comes out, tiny, in a white dress with two dark braids and grabs the back of a chair and says: "We lived with my grandmother . . . We rented an apartment . . . there was a tenant . . .

books . . . Grandmother pinned a dress to sew . . . And me, I felt sh-shame . . ."

Her life, *her* grandmother, *her* childhood, *her* "nonsense" . . . *Her* white nights.

The whole city knew Sonechka. People went to see *the* Sonechka. To see "Sonechka." "Have you seen her? She is tiny, in a white dress, with braids . . . Adorable!" They didn't know her name: "so small . . ."

White Nights[V] was an event.

The play was made up of three parts. The first was Turgenev's "Story of Lieutenant Ergunov." In this story, a young babe, somewhere in a suburban slum, bewitches an attractive young lieutenant. After all the promises and seductions, she vanishes—in smoke with his wallet. I recall at the beginning she waits for him, turns on the charm—and tidies herself and her home. The huge barn has a lone shoe in the middle. Lonely and worn-out. Suddenly, she rushes across the entire stage, turning on the charm!

This was not Sonechka but an introduction to Sonechka.

The second part? It seemed to be something about the sea, a harbor, sailors—maybe Maupassant: a brother and sister? It's over, disappeared.

Third part—curtain rises: a chair. Behind the chair, holding it, is Sonechka. She starts telling a story, confused yet smiling, about her grandmother, about the tenant, about their miserable life, about her young love. In this way, confused and smiling, with eyes sparkling and full of tears, like when she was at my place on Boris and Gleb Lane, telling me about our Yurochka—or about Evgeny Bagrationovich—without acting, or maybe seriously acting to death, but most of all, playing with the ends of her braids, never tying them with ribbons but playing with the hair itself, twisting it naturally—playing with the locks at her temples, brushing them away from her eyelashes, thus keeping her hands busy when they were longing for the back of the chair. These ends of her braids and locks at her temples—were all Sonechka's *little game*.

Even the dress she was wearing was not theatrical, not planned, but her summer dress, the one from when she was sixteen years old, perhaps was?

"I went to the Studio Three show and saw your Sonechka . . ."

And so she became to everyone my Sonechka—as *mine* as my silver rings and bracelets—or the apron with the rings that no one could dispute was mine and that no one but I would want.

It must be said here, because it will become obvious, that I immediately treated Sonechka as if she were a favorite object, a gift, with that feeling of joyful possession which I have never had before or since for a person—never—only for favorite objects. Not even for a favorite book, but for a ring, at last landing on just the right hand, glaringly, obviously—meant for me, bought from a gypsy—meant just for me, the ring that enjoys me as much as I enjoy it—and is close to me as I am to the ring, it could only be torn away from me along with my finger. Yes, the ring and my finger! I could never tire of this relationship: all the love, and my thoughts, that too.

One more thing: I was touched, irritated, insulted even, when they called her Sofia Evgenievna (like a grown-up!) or simply Gollidey (like a man!) or Sonya—they can't even make an effort to say Sonechka. But I saw that as a sign of indifference and even callousness. Even mediocrity. Didn't they realize she was Sonechka and nothing else, that saying otherwise would be rude—you can only speak to her with diminutive affection. When Pavlik called her Gollidey (having begun with Infanta!), I decided to distance myself from him. Not only Sonechka, but, in general, calling any woman (who is *not* a public figure) by her last name behind her back is a kind of familiarity, an abuse of power in her absence, a put down, turning her into a man. Calling her by her childhood name would be a sign of closeness and tenderness that cannot offend maternal feelings, of even an empress. (Amusing? I was two or three years older than Sonechka and I was upset for her like a mother.)

No, everyone who loved me: those who knew how to read me called her Sonechka—in my presence. With the polite addition of "your."

But while she is still before us, with her hands on the back of the chair, let's just focus on her appearance—to avoid any misunderstanding.

On the surface, with her eyelashes and braids, with all her scarlet and chestnut colors, she could have passed as a southerner, a Ukrainian girl, but only on the surface. There was nothing typical or traditional in that little face—she had a slender structure to her face—it was a masterpiece. I also want to say: this face was shell-like—in the way the ocean works a shell—from a scallop to the shell: the fold of the nostrils and the curve of the lips, the curl of the eyelashes, the ear! Her features carved precisely, poured freely—like they *worked* on it and *played* with it at the same time: not only had the Ocean worked on it but the wave played with it. I have never seen a pink pearl, but I am sure that her face was more pearl and more pink.

***

Where did she come from? When? In winter, she was not in my life. So it was in spring. In the spring of 1919, and not the very beginning but probably April, because connected with her in my mind are the feathery poplars in front of the house with their first few green leaves.

My first sight of her was on the sofa with her legs tucked, there was no light yet, just a bit of dawn in the window, and the first word of hers in my ears was a complaint: How frightened I was of you! I was afraid you would sweep him away. Because, Marina—on my knees!—not falling in love with you would have been unthinkable, impossible, simply (with astonished eyes)—stupid. That's why I couldn't come up to you for a long time, because I *knew* I would love you so much, you who he loved, and because of you he couldn't love me, and I didn't know what to do with this love of mine, because I *already* loved you from the first minute—there on the stage when you first lowered your eyes and read! Then—oh what a knife in my heart! What a knife!—when he came up to you, *at the end*, and you stood next to him at the edge of the stage, separated from everything, all alone. He whispered something to you, and you did not lift up your eyes—for he was speaking *only to you* . . . Really, Marina, I didn't want to fall in love with you! Now it's all the same to me, because he is nothing to me now. There's *you,* Marina, and now I see for myself that he was *not able* to love you, because if he did, he would not be repeating lines from "Saint Anthony"[VI] and he himself would become Saint Anthony, or if not Anthony, some other saint . . .

"Yuri."

"Yes, yes, and he would never offend, never eat dinner or breakfast. And now he's joining the Army."

"Like Saint George."

"Yes. Oh Marina. Exactly like Saint George, with a spear, like the ones on the gates of the Kremlin! Or else he would just *die* of love."

And just the way she said *die* of love, it was obvious she, too—would die of love for him—for me—and for everything; revolution or not, rations or not, Bolsheviks or not—it's all the same if she dies of love because it's her calling—her purpose in life.

"Marina, will you always love me? Marina, will you *always* love me, because you know I am going to die soon, I don't know why. I love life so much but I *know* that I could die soon, and that's why, that's why I am so *crazy and hopelessly* in love with all of it . . . When I say Yura—don't believe me. Because I know that in other places it's you . . . *You*, Marina, are not there—while they are! . . . Marina, did you ever think at this very minute, at this very moment, somewhere in a port town, on whatever island, a person you could love might come aboard? Or maybe disembark—for me it's always a sailor, a sailor—an officer or a simple sailor—who cares! . . . he might disembark and wander through the town looking for you, but you are here on Boris and Gleb Lane. Or maybe he just goes by Third Meshanskaya Street (so many sailors here in Moscow, so many, did you see? After five minutes—you're looking around like crazy!). But, you know, Third Meshanskaya Street is so far from Boris and Gleb Lane, like Singapore . . . (a pause). I only liked geography in school—of course, not all those latitudes and longitudes (I liked the meridians though)—I liked the names . . . And, Marina, the worst thing is that there are so many towns and islands, in the whole entire earth!—and a point only has the appearance of a point—the globe seems small at first and the little points—so many, thousands, thousands of little points to love . . . (I always used to say that to Yura, at the very moment I'd say that I didn't love anyone but him, I'd say that, Marina, in the same breath, the same giant breath, filled *with him, all of him,* because *that*'s true, too, *both* are—both are true, because it's all the same, I know that for a fact, but when I go to prove it—something is not right, like trying to reach the top branch when you need a little more height! At that point I think I'm going crazy . . .)

"Marina, who invented the globe? Do you know? I really don't know anything—not who made the globe, who made the map, nor who made the clock—What do they ever teach us in school??! I bless the person who invented the globe, (probably some old man with a long white beard . . .) so I can put my arms around the entire world all at once—with all my loved ones in it!"

***

". . . Or the clock . . ."

One day she was playing at the table in my home with an hourglass, a child's little five-minute hourglass: a glass vial framed in wood with the smallest waist—and through that little waist—the thinnest stream poured—of sand, a five-minute period of time.

"Look, already five minutes have passed . . ." Then silence, as if Sonechka was not in the room, and then suddenly, unexpectedly, she said: "Now the very last little grain will pass through! That's it!"

She played like this for a long time, her eyebrows wrinkling up, completely lost in that little stream! (And I in her). Suddenly there was a cry of desperation: "Oh Marina! I lost track. I suddenly started thinking deeply and so I didn't turn it over in time. Now I will never know what time it is. Because imagine if we were on an island, *who* would tell us? *How* would we know?"

"And say, a ship, Sonechka, would come to get coral from us? Pieces of coral? A pirate ship in which every sailor has three watches and six gold chains. Or even this: after a shipwreck—a cat has been saved with us. And I already know from girlhood, from childhood that the Chinese see time in the eyes of cats.

A missionary's watch stopped and he asked a boy on the street what time it was. The boy quickly ran off somewhere and came back with a huge cat in his arms, he looked him in the eyes and said: Noon."

"Yes, but wait, I was talking about that little trickle of sand that knows the time and wanted me to turn it over. Oh, Marina, I have the feeling I have killed someone!"

"You've *killed* time, Sonechka:"

What time is it? He is asked *here*
Strangely, he answered—Eternity.

"Oh what a miracle! What is this? Who is this he and did this *really* happen?"

"It was Batyushkov, the poet who went mad, and yes this really did happen."

"It's stupid to ask a poet the time. Useless. That's why he lost his mind—because of such stupid questions. Find yourself a watch! Tell *him* the time, don't ask him for it."

"No, it's not that—he was already suspected of being mad. They were just checking."

"And weren't they ashamed—his answer was that of a genius, a pure soul. But the question was from a medical student. A fool." (She rubbed the ball of her foot with her index finger) ". . . But Marina, imagine if I were God . . . no, no, wait—that instead of me, God was holding the hourglass and forgot to turn it over. I mean if he got to thinking about something for one second—and—then time, of course, was finished.

". . . What a frightening, miraculous little toy, Marina. I would like to take it to bed with me . . ."

***

A little trickle . . . little second . . . Everything for her was diminutive, her whole way of speaking. As if her petiteness somehow transferred to her speech. There were words—little words, birds in her words, perhaps an actor's, an actress's, an act, yet, oh my Lord, from her lips they sounded like something else! For example, *manerochka,* a little mannerism. "How I love your Alya; she has her own peculiar little mannerisms [*manerochki*] . . ."

Little mannerism (one step away from being *a little darling* "ma *chere*-ochka")—no, not an actress's but a boarding schoolgirl's word. And why does it always seem to reverberate in my ears: "When I was at the boarding school . . ." A regular high school was not only incapable of giving anything to her but of taking away from her—that old-fashionedness, that quaintness, century-old, 18th-century virginity, the urgency and that adoration, genuflection, or passion for tragic love.

A boarding school student, then an actress. Or perhaps, a schoolgirl, then a governess, and then an actress. (I remember vaguely that she spoke of other people's children . . .)

"Yesterday when Alya asked to stay up just a little longer, she made such a sweet little grimace . . ."

Little mannerism . . . little grimace . . . little second . . . little trickle . . . and she herself was . . . a *devochka,* a little girl, also diminutive.

***

"My father was a violinist, Marina. A *poor* violinist. He died in a hospital. I went to see him every day, I didn't walk away from him for one little minute. He was happy to be with me alone. I was always his favorite." (Does my memory deceive me? When I hear "court violinist"? What court? English? Russian? Because I forgot to mention Gollidey is an English name, a retelling of the English word: Holiday—the word for Sunday, festivity.

Sonya *Gollidey*: the name was tied to her like a little bell!)

"My sisters, Marina, are so beautiful. I have two sisters and both are beautiful. Tall, fair, blue-eyed—real ladies. It's me who's the ugly duckling, the black sheep (me) . . ."

Why they didn't all live together, I don't know. I only knew she was always preoccupied with their business and did so much for them. "I need lots of money, Marina, I need it so they can have *good* dresses and nice shoes for they . . . (with a deep sigh) . . . are stunning. They are tall, Marina, and slender. I'm the only one who's short."

"And you are so little, the youngest one, you should . . ."

"It's just because I'm so little. I need so little because I am no beauty, but the beautiful ones always—in all the fairy tales—always need a lot of things. Can't they dress like me!"

(A white blouse, black skirt, or a white dress—I don't remember seeing her in anything else.)

One time in a cafeteria, (dried fish soup, with pearl barley, the second course was just *vobla* [fish], no bread. Sonechka had given hers to Alya.) she pointed them out to me—they were sitting at a table, they nodded to her with their high English necks (then she ran towards them)— they were blue-eyed, porcelain faces, golden-haired, wearing white curved grand ducal hats . . .

"Look, Alechka, see the two ladies. They are my sisters. Aren't they gorgeous?"

"You're nicer."

"Oh, my dearest child! I'm nicer for you, because you love me."

"I love you because you are better than all the rest."

A child, disarmed by a child, she fell silent.

***

Going by the rule of fairy tales, clearly—and with my passion for names, this couldn't be explained otherwise—I never asked for their names. That's how they stayed in my mind—the sisters. Cinderella's sisters.

***

Sonechka's *Mother.* I remember her, too, being part of Sonechka's *world.* Write to mama. Send this to mama. No doubt she stayed in St. Petersburg, Sonechka's native city. (And her being in *White Nights* was no accident.) "You know, Marina, I used to walk there myself, I loved them [the white nights] so much . . . When I first read the play . . . I *never* really read it for the first time! But in *White Nights*, I am not only her, I am also him, the dreamer who has never really managed to escape the white night . . . I'm always two people, Marina, it's not I who split myself, but I am actually two: even in my love for Yura: I am me, and I am also him. Yura: I think all his thoughts, before he says them—I already know them (that's why I don't expect anything!)—it's funny for me to say this: when I'm him, I'm too lazy to love myself . . .

"Only with you, Marina, am I me, and still myself. And more than anything, Marina, I am everyone who, during the white nights, loves so much and walks and wanders. I myself am the white night . . ."

I knew she was from St. Petersburg right away, with her use of the word "ugly" instead of "bad"—the word used in Moscow.

"Isn't this ugly?"

"What?"

She says "ugly," and then she laughs.

Sonechka, a minor miracle. There's a rhythm.

Who and where
Miracle mile?

That's how Rosanette came up in my play *Fortuna* (Lauzun), so this is how the entire last scene of *Fortuna* came to be: Who and where?—and the whole idea for Rosanette (Sonechka) to be, Rosanette, the gatekeeper's daughter:

. . . I was sent here as a last wish.
Would you want to leave a letter for your family,
Maybe cut off a lock of hair for a keepsake.
Whatever it is you want, ask! What a day:
You can do *all* you want today!

Oh, how energetically Sonechka said the word *all*, an hour before execution, at this created hour, this ultimate hour of love, the ultimate hour that contains *all* love.

In this name—Rosanette.

(Sonechka! After my story, I wish all men would fall in love with you, that all wives were jealous, and that all poets would die for you . . .)

***

Sonechka and her plaintive exclamations began appearing in my journals after her first visit to me:

"Oh, Marina!" (This clever girl never used Ivanovna, [my patronymic] ever since *White Nights*.) Over and over, a thousand times, she'd say "I would love to play the Lady in the *Blizzard.* I know every move, every intonation, every break, every pause—*every* breath . . . No one, Marina, *no one* would play her like me, but I can't—I'm too petite . . ."

It was not about her height—not her size—others were just as small! Her small stature was quite ordinary—to play a fourteen-year-old girl—it was both her undoing and her charm that she was like this fourteen-year-old girl—*she was*. But she was actually nineteen. How many times—I'm not ashamed to admit—during our short time together did I regret she did not have an older, adoring, enlightened patron who would hold her with his aged arms, framing her in silver . . . And at the same time, like an experienced navigator, he could guide her . . . With my little boat—on a long voyage . . . But there were no such people in Moscow in 1919.

(I know, I know that with my love, I weaken the "impact," I know the reader wants to feel the love himself, but I am a reader, too, and I want to love too. I, like Sonechka, want to "love myself," like a dog. Maybe you haven't realized yet that my master is dead and I'm just howling, from afar and from years away?! I howl with grief—it's so simple!)

. . . Not the slightest feminine coquetry. Boyish bravado (with that very feminine physique, a young girl, a little girl), the mischievousness of an elf. She was everything that the Germans call "Einfall." (Sonechka, for you I'd steal three dictionaries! It's a pity I don't know English—I could find a lot for you there. And also—in Spanish!)

A series of images: Natasha Rostova on a flowery tub, "Kiss the doll!" . . . Natasha Rostova, hugging her knees, howling, like a dog, to the moon, from the windowsill . . . Ogarev's Consuela, saying goodbye to Herzen's Natasha at the stagecoach . . . Cosette with her doll and Fantine with Cosette . . . All those young girl images from Dickens, Juliet, Mireille, Mignon are finally gone, not even he: Mignon—the boy harpist, who became Mignon, who, after a kind of migration, was brought home to his mother by the young man who became Goethe.[VII]

(I know once again I'm not giving anything—but taking a lot—once I even crossed out this passage from my writing, but crowding me, overwhelming me, are the words, surrounding me, they so want to exist, through Sonechka again . . .)

I'm keeping one more secret, though. It will only come through in my poetry—no other way.

And so, because not one of my adult heroines could be "that little," I had to create little ones. Little girl characters: Rosanette in *Fortuna*, the girl in *The Adventure*, Francesca in *The End of Casanova*—and all of them are Sonechka, her, the real one, not the entire one, of course, because, in the words of Heine, the poet is not suited for theater and the theater is not suited for the poet—but she is always there, if not all of her, then it's always—her, never: anyone else.

However, I took one of my poems from her: from she who didn't write them, who never wrote a single line in her life. I, with my unparalleled boundless honesty, yes, I stole it. The only plagiarism in my life.

Once she was telling me about some grievance:

"Oh, Marina! And I had such big tears—bigger than my eyes!"

"You know, Sonechka, someday I'm going to steal this from you for my own poetry, because it is absolutely wonderfully accurate and . . ."

"Oh, go ahead and take it, Marina! Take whatever you want! Take everything I have into your poetry, take it all! Because everything will live in your hands—forever! What will be left for me? A few kisses . . ."

And so about three years later (who knows the day and time) this poem came:

The hour when my dear brother
And passed the elm for the last time

(With a pensive sigh: "Go back")
Tears bigger than his eyes.
The hour when my dear friend
Rounded the last cape
(With a pensive sigh: "Return!")
Waves bigger than his hands.

Hands away from the shoulders!
Lips keep following—to curse!
Speech has lost its sound,
Hand has lost its fingers.

At the hour when my dear guest . . .
—My Lord, look down upon us!—
Tears bigger than human eyes—
Human—and stars,
The Atlantic stars . . .

(The Atlantic stars twinkled above the town of Lacanau-Ocean, where I was writing my Story of Sonechka. Looking at them yesterday, after midnight, I remembered these lines. The opposite, though: above the ocean the *stars* were bigger than eyes! It has gone full circle.)

The poem was written and sent to Boris Pasternak, but the author and addressee was Sonechka.

And the last reflection, the echo of Sonechka in my writings—a long, long time after we had parted—in the chorus of my book *Swain*: "Marusya is the sweetest! (most beautiful of all, most ardent of all . . .)—Marusya herself, having risen like a flower, survived death itself, but she gives up her immortality so that she and her beloved could perish together."

***

"Marina, do you think God will forgive me? I have kissed so many!"

"Do you think God counted them?"

"I haven't even counted?"

***

. . . The most important thing is I am always the one who kisses first, as simply as shaking hands, only more irresistibly. I just can't hold back! Then, every time it's: "Who told you to do that? It's your fault!" I know perfectly well no one likes it, that they all like to bend down and beg, find the opportunity, court, chase after . . . But the most important thing is I can't stand it when someone else kisses me first. At least I am clear about when I really want it.

***

Marina, I could never understand (and I don't even understand myself) how, after just kissing—one can pray. With the very same lips . . . No, not the same! Whenever I prayed I never kissed anyone and whenever I kiss I never prayed.

Sonechka! Sonechka! *Your* lips kiss from the very depths of your heart.

***

We never kissed other than the hello and goodbye. But I often put my arms around her shoulders, with a feeling of protectiveness or like an elder. (I was three years older, essentially, my whole self was older. There was nothing "diminutive" or "little" about me.)

I embraced her fraternally.

It was a dry fire, pure inspiration, without any attempt at diffusing, expending, or igniting again. It was evil without remedies. I told this story, in French, to a friend of mine—fifteen years later. The friend has passed, but the story remains.

I don't remember kissing her other than the usual, almost mechanical kiss for hello and goodbye. It wasn't bad—or good. It wasn't about shyness; it was very much like using the informal "you;" I just loved her too much, everything else was less important.

Because a kiss, when you don't love—says so much, but when you do love—says so much less, and is not enough. Drink to drink once more. The kiss of love is like sea water for thirst. (Sea water and blood—good only for those in shipwrecks!) If it's already been said, I'll say it again. The important thing is not to say something new, it is to seek it alone and to tell the truth.

I prefer to keep my thirst.

One thing that, by virtue of its very simplicity, has never been written: the kiss in love is a bad path leading to forgetting the other. Leading from the beloved not to the beloved. Beginning by kissing a soul, we continue by kissing a mouth, and we finish with kissing—the kiss. Annihilation.

But I often embraced her with my arms, fraternally, protectively, to hide her a little from life, from the cold, from the night. It was the Revolution, so for a woman: it was life, it was cold, it was night.

. . . My little child who I never let return home alone.

I simply never thought about it—that there was this possibility between people like us. (This impasse.) It's only now, fifteen years later, that I think about it. I'm full of gratitude for not even having thought about it then.

***

Sonechka lived in her chair. It was deep, dense and green. A huge green chair that enveloped her, surrounded and embraced her like a forest. Sonechka lived in the green bush of the chair. The armchair was by the window, overlooking the Moscow River, with breathtaking views of the vast landscape.

Sitting there, she was consoled by Yura. Meanwhile she read—she read my little notes then she wrote me her own. She memorized her monologues while thoughtfully nibbling on a crust of bread, and after all the tears and notes, she'd carelessly drift to sleep with all the Yuras, the Vakhtangovs, and the others from the Studio . . .

It was her bed, her nest, her niche . . .

To get to Sonechka's, you had to go up a slight hill, toward the sound of the dam, past a crooked fence with an even more crooked inscription on the edge of its logs: "I am learning to write straight" (In 1919! As if there was nothing else to be concerned about! Yes—about such letters!)

There was a house. In the house was an armchair. In the chair was Sonechka, her legs folded under her as if the tide was rising. (A little more and she'll be submerged.) Her legs jump off and arms reach out to me:

"Marina! What a joy!"

Carefully she unloads my purse and shoulder bag from me. Sonechka doesn't need to be persuaded to seat me in her chair: she knows the firmness of my character and my habits. I sit at the window. The windowsill is low and wide. Behind me—free will. Behind my back—free will, before me—love.

"Marina! Today I went to early mass and I cried again so much" (busily counting on her fingers then folding them down on her palm): "Yura doesn't love me, Vakhtang Levanovich [Mcheldelov] doesn't love me, Evgeny Bagrationovich [Vakhtangov] doesn't love me . . . But he could! I could be his daughter, because I am Evgenievna[VIII]—they don't like me in that Studio."

"And what about me?!"

"Oh—you! Marina, you will *always* love me, not because I'm so great but you don't have time to stop loving me. But Yura has already stopped because I myself did not have time . . . to die."

Love, love. What was she thinking, always talking about love? . . .

This reminds me of one of my own questions, at that time, for a soldier of the former regiment of the Crown Prince, telling the story of when he saved the flag.

"How did you feel when you saved the flag?"

"But I didn't feel anything: if there's a flag, there's a regiment; no flag, no regiment."

(If there's love—there's life, if there is no love . . .

. . . For Sonechka loving was her being: *nonbeing* was in relation to another person: for her, loving was not a fulfillment of oneself in another person.)

She curled up into a ball, small, her face was not visible because of her hair, hands, tears, hiding deep within herself—from everything (like my daughter Irina's nanny Nadya from Vladimir used to say:)—she nestles. But all around—above and below—is the forest, the sky, the tides, in her chair.

The way she hoisted herself into it and pressed herself in, it was clear how much she needed someone to hold her in their strong, wide, loving, older hands. (After all, a chair is always an old man.)

Looking at Sonechka in the chair, you could guess her loving nature. (Nature is a word in her dictionary, strangely ancient, as if translated from Dickens.) For she pressed herself into the chair not like a cat in velvet, but like a living being into a living being.

I realized she was simply sitting on its lap!

To entertain her a bit and distract her from Yura, I told her how yesterday Alya and I walked to Vorobyovy Gory, and how, in the middle of the railway bridge, I watched the water through the iron crossbars, scared, and I sat down as Alya spoke to my fear with a story she made up on the spot: that the bridge had given way suddenly and she and I fell into the water but did not drown, because angels came to our aid at the last minute, and they took care of us. At the last moment they learned that this lady with a soldier's pack slung over her shoulder was a poet and the girl wearing officer's buttons was her daughter, then the angels carried us in their arms to the fair and took us for a ride on the carousel: "You, Marina, with your angel, were on a lion, and I, with mine on a ram . . ." and then these angels took us to Boris and Gleb Lane, and stayed to live with us and heated our stove and found us some firewood. "Because, you know, these angels were not angels. You, yourself, Marina, know *what* kind of angels they were . . ."

So with Alya's help, we crossed the bridge and really did ride on the carousel: me on a lion, she on a ram, and to reward her for the good experience of crossing the bridge I bought her a little raspberry gelatin dessert, and she ate it eagerly, like holy bread, and then we were transported across the river not by angels but by two men in red shirts, she recognized one as the beloved guide from *The Captain's Daughter* [by Pushkin]—and on and on. In response: Sonechka's sunshine face—her laughter—and radiance . . .

"Marina, I was acting in the provinces then. In summers there were always street markets—in the provinces. You know, I love all kinds of silly, cheesy stuff to death. The pink roosters, the wooden blacksmiths. I'd wear a kerchief. A pink one. When I'd put it on—well, I just felt like it was meant for me. But I had that feeling about everything, everything: the kerchief, my sisters' huge white hats. There were times I thought: why not put on a crown! But no, it would fall off: after all, I had a terribly small head: ridiculously small—no, no, not that! This *hair*, try shaving it off! I tell you: there would be *nothing*!

"Marina, would you love me if I shaved off my hair? But you already love me—with my hair shaved. Everyone shaves for you, even Yurochka, no, he only partly shaved like a prisoner!—Marina, am I talking too much? Inappropriately, yes, and a lot, about everything at once, everything all at once? You know, there's not a moment I don't want to talk, even when I'm crying: when I sob, I talk to myself! Even in my sleep I talk all the time: I argue, I talk, I chatter, in a stream over stones—a bunch of nonsense, Marina! Nobody listens to me. Only you. Ah, Marina! The first man I loved was much older than me, more than twice my age, he already had grown children—that's why I loved him—and he was *very* indulgent, never got angry, but he often reproached me jokingly: 'Ah, Sonya! Don't you know that there are times you don't *need* to talk?'

"But me," she continued, "I never stopped talking. Everything all at once comes to my head—so many different things. I sometimes regret that I only have one voice at a time. Guess what, Marina, I'm going to tell you about a ventriloquist!'"

(Yes, she talked terribly much. The Tsarina's favorite words in her Tobolsk letters were: "Children babble like waterfalls . . .")

". . . So—about that street fair. Once I was walking along in my kerchief and peeking from under it I suddenly saw: a huge woman, a peasant woman, a grandma in a short crimson sequined skirt dancing—to the sound of a barrel organ. A clerk was turning the barrel organ. Already middle-aged but kind of immature, with a red nose and a badge. (Even his nose looked like a badge.) I felt terribly sorry for him—poor thing! must have been thrown out of his office for drunkenness, he looked hungry . . . Well, it turned out it was because of love, Marina. He had seen her at a fair ten years ago, in his hometown, and she was young and thin and must have been terribly appealing. He immediately fell in love with her (but she didn't with him, because she was married already—to a ventriloquist), and every morning he'd come to the fair, and when the fair left town, so did he, and he'd follow her everywhere. He was fired from his position, and then began to turn the barrel organ and has been spinning it for ten years, and did not notice that she had gotten fat—no longer beautiful, even frightful . . . It seems to me that if he'd only stop turning, he'd have understood everything right away—and then died.

"Marina, I did something terrible: you know, that woman never kissed him the whole time—because if she had kissed him even once, he would have stopped grinding that organ: he was grinding for that kiss!—Marina! I said this to him in front of everyone, my heart pounding. I said: 'Don't be angry, please, I know your story: I know how you left everything for love. I'm the same myself . . .'—And right in front of everyone, I kissed him. On the lips.

"But Marina, I had to push myself, I didn't want to, it was awkward and scary: I was afraid of him, and of her, too. I simply didn't want to! I immediately said to myself: first, the fair is leaving tomorrow. Second, today is the last day. Third, no one ever kissed him in his life. Fourth, and won't kiss him. Fifth, you always say that there is nothing more important than love. Sixth, now prove it. And *yes*, Marina, I kissed him! It was the only difficult kiss in my entire life. But if I hadn't kissed him, I could never have played Juliet."

"And what about him?"
"Him?" (With a big laugh),

Standing as if thunderstruck
was Evgeny . . ."
[from Pushkin's Eugene Onegin]

"And, I didn't even look at him. I went on without turning around. He may still be standing there. Ten years after, ten years of dirty squares and drunken men, and I kissed him—and I wasn't even the right one!

"And here's another story, Marina, about a sailor named Pasha . . ."

"Here's the story about Pasha the sailor. In my spring 1919 journal there's only this entry: 'Sonechka Gollidey's story about the sailor Pasha'—next to it there are some empty pages to write something that wasn't written. The sailor Pasha is not there! Lost at sea, the sailor Pasha has gone off somewhere!"

Oh, what an armchairful of stories, confessions, admissions, horrors, and consolations . . .

The second figure in Sonechka's room was a chest, a red leather one, from way back when Sonechka's father was a court musician. "Sonechka, what's in it?" "My dowry! (we'll find out more later about the dowry). Someday I will definitely get married! In the most serious way: with a proposal, a refusal, an agreement, a white dress, a corsage, and a veil. I would hate getting married in civilian clothes! Just like that, walking in, after hastily brushing my teeth, and then announcing it a month later: 'We've been married for a year.' That's no good. Because I have to feel the confusion first, then clink glasses, and let the champagne flow freely, and then I want to be congratulated, to have presents, and most importantly—to cry! Oh, how I want to cry, Marina! For my Yurochka, for Evgeny Bagrationych, for the Theater, for everything, everything, because then it would be over: I would only love him."

The third character in Sonechka's room was order. Unimaginable, impossible during the Revolution. As if there were three maids working, sweeping, and picking things up! Not one little thing, not one little speck, nothing was moved. Not a single little note (not mine nor Yura's). Or were they all under a pillow? The room was that of a schoolgirl on vacation, of a governess on duty, a room that was a hundred, no—two hundred years old. Or even simpler—like a sailor's cabin: a kind of order that showed a presence, not an absence. Order lived in the room. A midshipman standing at attention.

And no one worked on it. Maryushka [the servant] stood all day in line waiting for *vobla* [dried fish] and vegetable oil (another thing that will be discussed later!). And upon her return, she'd hit the wall with the fish. Everything—with Sonechka, was done by hand and in person.

So I was especially touched by her friendship with me, her sincere admiration for my crazy, weird house—where everything was being moved around—forever and ever, on and on, nonstop moved, farther and farther—until things went out beyond the walls—was it a boon? looted? or sold off?

I will add that children, especially those from good homes, have always liked my house (the same to this day), its boundless freedom and constant surprises, and miracles appearing beneath one's feet—a gigantic box with an abyss at the bottom, an infinite supply of more and more things, often—with no name.

Sonechka liked my home as a *child*, like the fourteen-year-old she was.

To sum up my house: it was Dickensian, *The Old Curiosity Shop*, where people slept on stilts, or like in *Oliver Twist*—on sacks. Sonechka herself was right out of Dickens: Little Dorrit in the debtor's prison and Copperfield's Dora with her account book and dog pagoda and Florence with her brother Dombey in her arms, and that strange girl from *Our Mutual Friend*, luring the old Jewish man to the roof—so as not to be invisible: "Montez! Montez! Soyez mort! Soyez mort!"—and the one from *Tale of Two Cities* who played the harpsichord, with the moss being blown around by a thunderstorm and the clatter of footsteps of revolutionary crowds and the sound of the first drops of rain . . .

It was all because I met Sonechka—that all the Dickens' girls were there.

Sonechka's appreciation for my home was a cry from the ancestors: atavism.

***

(Early Dostoevsky rewriting Dickens, when Dostoevsky was like Gogol: that's my Sonechka. *White Nights* had three authors. My Sonechka's role was written by three writers.

How could she go wrong playing in *White Nights*?!)

***

I always came to see her in the morning—I'd walk in, run in alone, without my children. I always remember her room as radiant—as if there had been no night in the room. The gold of the sun on the green of the chair and the green of the chair on the dark gold of the parquet floor.

Oh, Sonechka, if only someone could take you and the chair and transport you to another life. And place the chair there, without removing you from it, right into the middle of the eighteenth century—your century, when women were not expected to have masculine principles, and the world was content with feminine virtues and did not demand ideas—but rejoiced at feelings, and rejoice at the kisses that now you'd scare people off with, in 1919.

Would that those two square stiff iron-like things not hang down from your chair, but instead tiny delicate shoes that should not step on the Moscow cobblestones, that they not walk at all, and that their soles be like that of a child who has not yet walked.

You (I was looking for the right word for you—precious object? jewel? gem? *joyau? bijou?)—Kleinod!* [Gem] But no one in 1919 Moscow saw this except for me, who could do nothing for you.

***

"Oh, Marina! I was so ashamed in front of him—my low, square, blunt-nosed feet!"

This time she said in front of "him"—not in front of Yura. Sonechka came into my life at the same time as my immense grief for: the passing of Alexey Aleksandrovich Stakhovich, in the first days after his death. Who Alexey Alexandrovich Stakhovich[IX] was for me—I have already said elsewhere, here I will quote my unpublished poem for him:

Look at those callouses—you can't hide three centuries!
You can't straighten your hands—axing them off!
Oh, you, most treasured of all treasures:
My kind! My breed!—I know you.

You hover over a black frying pan smoking.
All around—your Versailles is hushed.
Even with the most skewed peasant shirt
You can't shorten your neck!

Bending over a pile of snow or soot
Still *proud* is your arched back!
Not with shouts, but with lordly blessings
Was your work given to you.

Do your trading with the Arbat down-and-out
A worthless herring for a packet of cigarettes

A hooked nose denounces equality:
Your nose is hooked and he is snub-nosed.

If, suddenly, you tire of getting paid,
And a child gives you a flower—in homage,
You would kiss that little hand
As you once did—the empress's palm.

One of the listeners says: What does it mean—tires of getting paid (a look of incomprehension)—when a person gets tired of being paid? Maybe tired of selling? But does that happen? (Me, happily:) And how! It happened to Leo Tolstoy who was tired of receiving income from Yasnaya Polyana, and for Count L. N. Tolstoy's writings and went to the fields. This is an exceptional case, a genius, whereas with you it is about a "child." My "child" is a woman, and to receive is only a question of patience, and women are more patient than geniuses. That's why my "child" immediately offered a rose to Stakhovich . . .

Second Poem

Oh noble Russian, let the bakeries shut down
With their seven locks and the stoves freeze over—
while you with your dignified gait and straight shoulders,
You step forth into your grave.

With the old world ablaze and fate fulfilled—
"Nobleman, make way for the woodcutter."
Around you—eighteenth century in the air
As the rabble, yes the rabble, keeps flourishing

Meanwhile roofs are being torn from palaces
And the rabble is tearing up coveted booty.

And while the world is being destroyed, you keep
Teaching "manners, deportment, and conduct."

You did not go out to offer the rabble bread and salt
And cross yourself like a bored gentleman!
In the dark kingdom of toiling calloused hands
There were your exquisite hands.

(It is not up to me to despise calloused hands, unless I despised myself first—but at that time, the love of callouses was imposed and it became an obligation to love them. Hence my feeling of hatred.)

I will also add that Sonechka and Stakhovich worked in the same studio—the Second Studio—where they were putting on Sonechka's *White Nights* with Sonechka being the only character and also *The Green Ring*[X] with Stakhovich being the only character (ring means youth).

***

It was precisely his "manners, deportment, and conduct"—instructions that Sonechka told me about when she mentioned her blunt-toed shoes.

"Such a shame, Marina! I'd get red every time! For example, he'd explain how a woman has to greet, bow, extend her hand, say good-bye to someone, or, conversely, receive them."

"Got it? Then—let someone demonstrate. There was no one! Well, then, you go ahead—Gollidey, Sonya."

"So I went, Marina, burning with shame because of my coarse, low, terrible shoes with bull noses. Walking in those shoes, crossing the entire hall—in front of him, he who had danced at court balls all over the world and was used to pumps and small feet."

O feet, little feet, where are you now,
There—trampling spring flowers?
[from Pushkin's Eugene Onegin]

"But I got up and walked, Marina, because no one else could do it, the others were even worse. It's not that they were dressed worse, but . . . well, they didn't know anything at all: how to reach out their hands, how to escort a guest out. Oh, and I wouldn't know how to do all this, Marina, if it weren't for these old shoes! How well I knew how to do all this deeply, deeply, since birth! I knew right away!

"And he always complimented me, maybe just to console me about these terrible shoes?—Yes, that's it—exactly . . . and he never even looked at them, as if he didn't see them, or that they pained me. I didn't look at them either. I was only afraid before he said: 'You, Gollidey, Sonya!' And when he said that I just walked so easily, I never gave them another thought—oh, Marina! I didn't lower myself to them anymore.

"He, of course, noticed them, because when one of our students complained that she couldn't do it because the shoes were 'too heavy'—Stakhovich: 'Whatever the shoes, the gait remains. Look at Sofia Evgenievna: who would say she had a leaden weight on each foot, like Byron's prisoner Bonivard'"[XI]

"Sonechka, do you know the fairy tale of the Little Mermaid?"

"You mean the one who danced on steel blades? But that's a thousand times easier than on these flat irons! Because these are really like irons . . . That's my favorite fairy tale, Marina! Every time I read it, I feel like her. How she wanted to come to the surface—and how when she surfaced, she saw the world above, and that marble boy who turned out to be dead . . . and the prince, and how she brought him to life, and then lost her speech, and then the mute mermaid danced in front of him on those blades.

Oh, Marina, it is the highest bliss—to love like that, to love like that . . . I would give my soul just to give my soul!

"Oh, Marina! How I love to love! I love you madly—I myself love to love! From morning, till the next morning, and I love the morning—to sleep in longer . . . and already know, that again I'll . . . Do you ever forget when you love—that you love? I never do. It's like a toothache—only the opposite, the opposite of a toothache, it still aches there, but here there's no word for it. (she thinks: does it sing?) Well, it's like sugar, it's the opposite of salt, but just as strong. Ah, Marina! Marina! Marina! They're all complete imbeciles! (I'm astonished:—But who?)—Those who don't love, they don't love themselves, that's the point—as if it were necessary for them to love you. I'm not saying . . . Well, you know—you get tired—our heads against the wall. But you know, Marina (in a mysterious tone), there is no wall *I* would not break down! After all, Yurochka too . . . there were times he had *such* loving eyes! But he—I have this feeling—he just didn't have the strength to say the words, it would be easier for him to move a mountain than to say them. It's not that he had no support, but beyond was another mountain, and another mountain, and another mountain . . . a whole Himalaya of love, Marina! Do you see, Marina, how all of them, the ones who kiss, the ones who pretend to love, all of them are afraid to say the word, it's why they never say it?! Someone explained once to me this was well, rude . . . (giggles:) old-fashioned. Why words, when there were actions? (i.e. kissing and so on). And I said to him, 'Well! No! Actions don't prove anything, but a word is everything.' That's all I need from a person: *I love you*, and nothing more, they can do whatever else, then let him do whatever, let him not love me, I don't believe in actions, if the words—the words are there. I fed myself on the words, Marina, that's why I became so thin.

"Oh, Marina, how greedy, calculating, and cautious they are! I always want to say: 'Just say it.' I won't check up on you. But they don't because they think it's about getting married, getting involved, and not being able to unbind. If I am the first one to say [I love you], I would never be the first to leave. (They wouldn't even say it after me, Marina, not one.) For sure I would not be the first one to leave!

"Marina! Never was I the first one to leave. In life—as long as God lets me have it—I would never be the first to leave. I just cannot. I always wait for the other one to leave first, I do everything possible to make the other leave, because for me it would be easier to become a corpse. (What a horrible word. Completely dead. You know: it's the dead person no one has ever loved. But for me, Marina, there is no dead person like that!) Even within myself I was never the first to leave. I was never the first to stop loving. I'm always there to the end, to the very last drop—just like when a child drinks something. Even though it may be an empty glass—you sip, sip, until you're left with your own breath!

"Oh, you know, you'll laugh—it was a brief encounter—during a tour—it doesn't matter who it was—a young one—but I fell madly in love with him, because every evening he sat in the front row—very *poorly* dressed, Marina! He didn't sit there for the money, but because he wanted to see me, and on the third evening he looked at me so hard that his eyes almost popped out onto the stage or like he himself was about to jump up on stage. (I would be talking, moving, acting, and I'd glance sideways: and, what? No, he'd still be sitting there.) You have to understand! It wasn't the usual loving, devouring male gaze (he was almost a boy)—he was drinking me in, Marina, he was bewitched, and it was as if with every word and every movement I made I was pulling him in—like on a noose—a rope, a line—pulling him in, reeling him in—mermaids know this feeling—and violinists, or rather their bows know—and also rivers . . . And fires, Marina! Something is about to leap at me—as if to throw me into a fire. I just didn't know how I'd finish my play. Because I, Marina, all the time had the feeling I would trip and fall into those eyes.

"And when I was with him, finally, backstage (I know this is terribly vulgar, but *everything* is vulgar, isn't it? Even the *rocks* where D'Annunzio's *virgins* sat!) . . . but that pathetic backstage is where I kissed him. I felt nothing, just one thing: I was saved!

"It was terribly quick. We had nothing to talk about. At first I kept talking, talking, talking, and then I fell silent. Because I couldn't, it was impossible, I—I couldn't allow any response to my words—only looks, only kisses! And so lying down in the morning, before the morning, when I was still asleep, I began to wake up, I suddenly noticed that I was repeating something over and over, yes, my lips, words. Then I listened, and you know what it was I was saying: please me just a little bit more, please me just another little minute, a second more, please!—And then what?

"No—*he couldn't.*—What?—Please me again. He couldn't have even if he'd heard me. Because don't believe it: it wasn't really him that I was begging, him, sleeping—we didn't even live together, we lived in different places, and really—I was begging the air, perhaps—asking God, it was an incantation, Marina, for myself, so that I could hold on a little longer.

"And, then? (eyes beaming)—I held on. He could not, but I could. He never knew. It was exactly right. A very strict father, a general in Moscow, never knew I was an actress: I supposedly was living with a friend (what if he was capable of pursuing me, playing the fool?)—I'll never forget (no lie), when the train started moving—(I never kiss people in public)—but I kissed *his roses through* the train window. Because, Marina, that's well and good, but justice is justice. It's not his fault I don't like him anymore. This is not a fault, but a problem. It was not *his* fault if he no longer pleased me, it was *my* problem, my weakness. Like breaking a china service then getting angry that it wasn't made of steel.

"And the play—during which we fell so in love with each other—was by Yuri Slezkin.[XII] Funny name? But right for me. Even our manager told me: 'Little Sonechka, you are always in tears, if only you could marry Yuri Slezkin.' (Busily:) Do you even know, Marina, that he's an old man?"

(I know that I am breaking the narrative, but honor is higher than art.)

This "Please me again, please!" is my second plagiarism.

Like that consumptive woman
Moaning during the night: Please me again!

And further:

Like that consumptive woman
Asking everyone: *again*, just a little more!
Please me!

And—finally:

Like the one with her sailor— you,
Making a bargain with life: *another* minute
Please me!

So, Sonechka's plea is preserved, through poetry, and told over and over to the end. For if Sonechka were older, that's precisely how she would have ended.

***

"Well, Sonechka, about Stakhovich. Besides taking bows, what else were these lessons about?"

"About everything. For example—how to do my hair. A woman's hair must be preserved—respecting the shape of the head. Not overly raised, the hair should only—and precisely—frame the face, so that the face becomes the most important thing. It should be parted in the middle and smoothly combed back, partly covering the ear: like you do—Gollidey, Sonya—said Aleksey Aleksandrovich (Stakhovich). 'But my hair is not very smooth!' I said, smiling. 'Yes, but you have natural ringlets, a natural wave, and the framing is there, it's just—a little—rococo. I'm mean the general line: yours is simple—marvelous. Quite marvelous.' (Oh, Marina, How proud I was at those moments! Because I felt: he distinguished me not only from those ahead, but from those *behind us*!) . . . Also about what to do, for example, if my stocking starts to fall down while walking on the street or if somehow it gets unfastened, he'd say: 'Whoever you are walking with, calmly move away and without haste, without any fuss, correct and fix the problem. Don't pull anything, don't rush, don't hide: calm-ly, calm-ly. Okay . . . Show me, Gollidey! You and I are walking along the Arbat, and you feel like your stocking is coming down, and in three more steps it will completely fall—What would you do?'

"And—I'd show him. I'd move away a little to the side, bend over, feel for the elastic band and calm-ly, calm-ly . . .

"'Bravo, bravo—Gollidey, Sonya! If you are, indeed, with *some* companion, and not just with me' (and he had such a wonderfully pitiful, mocking smile, Marina! . . . your old teacher . . . he had such composure . . .)

"One day I couldn't resist asking: 'Alexey Alexandrovich, how do you know all this: about falling stockings, shoelaces, our feelings, our heads? How do you know us so well—from head to toe?' And he replied seriously (so seriously that everyone would believe him, but not me): 'I know everything and it is not surprising; I'm an old man, but where do you, a young girl, get such questions?' It was always me who did the demonstrating and me who was the example, others were shown the things you're *not* supposed to do, and me—what I'm supposed to do. That's why the kids called me: Stakhovich's model."

"Did the girls envy you?"

Triumphantly she said: "They were bursting with joy!! It was really such an honor! We all loved him extremely much, and if you only knew what kind of dolls we had. And on top of that, they were sassy and full of themselves! And what accessories! (giggles)—*They* had real ladies' shoes."

"But why, Sonechka, did you earn so little?"

Meekly, she said: "Other people had husbands, Marina. Some had one, and some two. I only had Yura. And my mother. And two sisters. They were . . ."

"The beautiful people. I know and I've seen them. And you were Cinderella, who had to shake off your cinders, while the other ones dance. But weren't you the actress?"

"But they were older. No, Marina, after my father's death I immediately understood—I knew what I had to do.

"But I still hated *them*—those old shoes (shows her foot). How many tears they cost me! I never got used to them."

***

"Marina! It was awful. He first came to the Moscow Art Theater after he had typhoid—and no one recognized him. They just passed him by and didn't even recognize him, he had changed so much and aged so much. Then he said to one of the students: 'I'm nothing more than a useless old man.'

"But how he sang! Marina! He had such a superb voice!"

(We were sitting upstairs in the empty wood-paneled kitchen, the children were sleeping, and the moonlight . . .)

It was a waltz—old-fashioned and slow
(Abruptly, as if placing a period)
And—wonder-ful!

Ah if I were—young again
How I would have loved you!

"Aleksey Aleksandrovich! Is that really you! That's not in the song!" we'd protest, laughing.

"In mine, yes."

***

Alexey Alexandrovich—you who knew the value of women, of pearls, of serfs—why did you not fall in love with my Sonechka, and love her more than your own soul? After all, "the air of the eighteenth century" surrounded her. What did you need to survive that terrible March? Why was it impossible for you to endure one more hour?

And there she was beside you—full of life, charming, so ready to love you and die for you—she who was dying without love.

Maybe you were thinking: she has a lot of young ones after her . . . But come on, I know what they were like! You too, for that matter!

How could you leave her—to all of them, to every one of them, to any of those boys you were uselessly teaching deportment, manners, etc.

There was one among them . . . But we'll talk about him—later.

***

At the theater, they didn't like her: they were unfair to her. I often complained about this to my friend Vakhtang Levanovich Mchedelov (her director, the one who discovered Sonechka for Moscow).

"Marina Ivanovna, don't believe that she is so difficult. She's not just capricious but impossible. You never know how she will respond to a comment. And sometimes she's inappropriate (deeply melancholic)—you tell her something, and she looks right into your eyes and laughs. Yes, she laughs so hard that you have to start smiling. And then it's over. The illusion is over. What do you do? Oh, and she's not at all ambitious but she does what she wants, like a tyrant: *she* knows what she needs—and—she doesn't listen."

"Or maybe she does really know—and you have to do as she says."

"Well, then she needs her own theater. We have a studio, it's collective work, we try different things. We work together."

"And what if she's already made it, done it all?"

"Hmm . . . In *White Nights* for instance. She acts as herself; it's her height, her voice, her laughter, her tears, her braids. Yes, she's exceptionally gifted, but I still don't know whether it's really a talent—or just being human—or a woman. She was everything—too exceptional. An exception can't fit into an ensemble: she stands out too much!"

"Give her leading roles!"

"It's not always possible. True, she is not suitable for every role—for physical reasons—she is so petite. She needs special staging: and putting her in the middle of the stage—that's all. Like in *White Nights.* She knew everything, wanted everything and could do everything herself. What is a director to do? (I, to myself: Just go along with it and appreciate her.) And, besides, we are a studio, it's only right, there are elementary rules of fairness. This actress is from a Western theater, not a Russian theater. It would be necessary to write plays especially for her . . ."

"Vakhtang Levanovich, you have a marvel in your hands."

"But what do I do if it's not what I need?"

"If you don't need it—give her to someone else!"

"But who?"

"I would say, quoting your allegation: present her to—the eighteenth-century hands of the young melancholic English patron who would carry her in his arms whenever he was not on his knees before her. What does she lack? Just go back two centuries and get two loving, powerful arms—and let her have her own theater—in a pink shell. Don't you see that she is a child actress, an actress in a golden carriage, a birdlike actress? A Malibran, an Adeline Patti, a hummingbird, not an ordinary member of your Second or Third Studio? You need to *adore* her and not *offend* her?"

"But no one has offended her, she herself offends! You don't know how mean she can be, she snaps, she's prickly, she's gruff, and you can't take her anywhere. She may be a wonderful soul, but she has a terrible character. Marina Ivanovna, don't be upset but you barely know her—you may know her poetically, or like a human being, in her home by herself, with you, but there is her professional life, a need for comradely behavior. I'm not saying she is a bad comrade. She's not any kind of comrade, she's independent. Do you know how Stanislavsky[XIII] talked about being part of the circle? Well our Sonechka is the complete opposite—she is the embodiment of leaving the circle. Or maybe—smack in the middle of it.

"And she has a terrible way of speaking. You only have to make fun of her a little and she starts crying. Cries and then says something horrible to you. Sometimes you think: Is she a child? A woman? A demon? She can be a real demon."

(For a moment it dawned on me. People don't talk like this about those they don't love. They talk like this about the ones they love, about something hopeless, about someone they used to love! But no one spoke about her any differently and for everyone she was a problem: they didn't love her, she tormented them like a thorn in the flesh.)

***

"Marina, a great misfortune has befallen me today!"

"Is it our angel again?"

"No, this time it's not him, it's the opposite! They decided to put on *The Four Devils* and they didn't even give me one of them, not even the fourth one! Not even the smallest one! Not even the fifth!"

(Then she said the most memorable thing: "I had the most enormous tears—bigger than my eyes!")

***

Yes, they thought she was nasty. They didn't say it to my face because they thought I was nastier, but in response to my being softened by her kindness—they remained silent or grumbled. Yet I have never seen such kindness more simple, more obvious, more open in a being. She gave everything she had, understood everything, pitied everyone. And saying she's nasty?—it was like me with Khodasevich,[XIV] sometimes there would be a question, or an answer, or even better still a quick linguistic response, a *surrender* to language. Or a retort—like a cat's paw.

A model young woman—a good little demon. All of my little Sonechka—like the Countess of Segur [a French writer born in Russia]. We are not compatriots for nothing!

(The Countess of Segur was a great writer who was foolish enough to imagine herself a grandmother and wrote only for children. Take a look at her *New Fairy Tales* [Bibliothèque Rose]—her best but least known work—they are quite exceptional, because they are completely original [not a single imitation of any known folk tale]. Tales I have been faithful to for more than three decades, fairy tales I have already gifted to people in Paris four times and I still have three, because when I see them in the store window—I just can't help but buy them).

***

A few concluding words about Vakhtang Levanovich Mchedelov. He deeply loved poetry and was a true friend, a person of true compassion, and I infinitely preferred him to the brilliant Vakhtangov (Sonechka's Evgeniy Bagrationych). I felt from him a kind of cold wind of intellect and even extravagance—the coldness and sterility of the word extravagance. (In terms of the theater I may be mistaken, but in a human sense—I am not.) And if there was something Vakhtang Levanovich could not do for my Sonechka, it was because that *something* was *everything*. That is, it signaled a complete annihilation of himself, nonexistence, love. From a social point of view, a gross injustice, Vakhtang Levanovich was undoubtedly better than me, but I loved Sonechka more than he did. Vakhtang Levanovich loved the Theater; I preferred Sonechka. Why couldn't he give her "at least the smallest role, the fifth devil"—those devils were not real but allegorical, and not devils at all? (I doubt that on stage, with four acts in a row—there would be four tails on stage at once.) I don't know this play, I believe—it's taken from Herman Bang's circus novel *The Four Devils*. I was sad about the *word* itself. And—the tears.

***

No, they did not love my Sonechka. The women—because of her beauty; the men—because of her intelligence; the actors (male and female)—because of her talent; all the others—because of her weirdness: the danger of her weirdness.

The women find her ugly
But the men are crazy about her . . .

Yes, to the first line (that is to say, as in poetry, just the opposite), the second—no. At the very height of her beauty and talent and passion, not one of them loved her; they spoke of her with a little laugh—and a little fear.

For the men, she was dangerous, like a child—a creature, not a woman. They didn't know how to deal with her. They didn't understand her . . . (Sonechka's mind never went to sleep. "One little eye, go to sleep, the other one, too," but the third one never went to sleep.) All were afraid that (when her tears came!) she would be laughing at them. When I remembered *who* they preferred to my Sonechka, what false, artificial creatures, what counterfeits they were—from the pseudo Beatrices to the pseudo Carmens (let's not forget we live in the very heart of pretense: the theater).

By the way, she seemed more Spanish than English, and so she had nothing national about her—to protect her from being questioned about her obvious southern Little Russian nationality [Ukrainian]—the most typical ethnicity. The Spanish woman's face is the least national, the most generally human face in its social aspect and harmony: yet the most unique—from portrait to allegory, the Spanish woman's face is the female face with all its potential for suffering and passion, that is—Sonechka's face.

She was geographically a Spaniard, not operatically. A Spanish street girl, a worker at a cigar factory. Spin her around in the middle of a square in Seville and she'll be in her element. It's not for naught that I, in the heat of the moment, without thinking, brought her into one of my first poems: "Little Cigar Girl!" And even better: Consuela—or Conchita—Concha. Concha—is almost Sonechka! "Oh yes Marina! Oh no, Marina! Concha—it's almost like the word [in Russian] for "will end"!

It's not a coincidence that the first thing I heard about her was Infanta. (From Infanta to cigar girl, the Spanish woman's face, a classless face.)

Now that Spain is closer to us, Spain has truly moved closer, while the false Spain has moved away. When every day we see dead and living faces of women and children, we can come upon Sonechka's. With one exception, it is a unique face.[XV]

I just have to add one more thing: such small faces sometimes flourish among the petty bourgeoisie. They flourished among the Russian petty bourgeoisie, in Turgenev's time. (Late Turgenev suffered a backlash.) A muslin curtain and behind it—huge black eyes. (Where do they come from? All his relatives were blonde.) The younger sisters had such faces—the seventh, the sixth, the last. "The postmaster had six daughters, the seventh is a beauty."

In the suburbs, in the backyards, on the outskirts . . . where the ends don't meet, they diverge.

Earrings—would suit this little face.

***

And also hazelnuts. Sonechka had a passion for hazelnuts, and of all the food deprivations, she missed them most of all. And with her laughter, and her teeth, and her speech too, it's as if the nuts were being nibbled on and rolled around in her mouth—like squirrels shuffling around in bins.

"So green and sour to the bite, the sourest thing there is—more than a lemon! Tart like a green apple! And suddenly—the nut itself: creamy, slightly dark, and pop! Split in two, as if cut with a knife—the meat! so round, so hard, it's the hardest thing there is! Two halves: one for you, one for me. But I don't only like the wild hazelnuts. (And picking them, Marina! There they are at the very top—a whole bunch of them, and another bunch, and another—and you just can't reach them. You bend, bend the branch—suddenly!—it breaks!—and then swings back and forth—and the blue sky—so blue that your eyes burn! So green your eyes hurt! They're like stars, Marina! Shells—with rays of light!) I love the ones that grow in the city: the cashews, the American walnuts, and the cedar pine nuts—such wonderful little African ones! A whole bag! And I love reading *War and Peace*. I love the Peace part, Marina, not the War part—it's all so arbitrary. I always skip pages and pages—because it's about men, Marina, not us . . ."

. . . The scattered hazelnuts, the streams over pebbles—water trickling over pebbles and pebbles under trickles of water—the chattering leaves ("wind leafing through the birch pages"); and the gentle clasp of a handful of pearls; and green leaves of lilies of the valley—even the shower of tears!—all that is round in nature and everything that moves and laughs in nature, and all that makes nature laugh made Sonechka laugh. But since it was all at once—the leaves, the water, the seeds, the nuts, along with her white teeth and dark eyes, all of it together gave rise to something incomparably sumptuous in nature . . .

—in a word:

I will never tire of listening to the chatter
I'll never tire of kissing those little feet . . .

Men didn't love her. Women didn't either. *Children* loved her. Old people. Servants. Animals. Very young girls.

Everything, everything was given to her so that she could be loved madly, to the point of losing her soul, on her knees: talent, ardor, beauty, intelligence, indescribable charm, and nameless glory—better than a name ("the one in—*White Nights* . . .") All this, in her hands, was only dust, because she really wanted—to love herself. She loved herself.

Sonechka would have needed a great poet. A great poet, that is—as great a person as he was a poet. She never met one of those. Maybe it could have been one of the first two hundred volunteers of 1918 [White Guards] in Novocherkassk, any one of the two hundred. But they were no longer in Moscow by 1919. They were—nowhere.[XVI]

***

"Oh, Marina! I loved them so! How I wept over their fate! I even prayed for them! You know, Marina, when I love—I'm not afraid of anything, I don't even feel the ground beneath my feet! Everyone was saying to me: Where are you going! You'll get killed! There's gunfire, it's the height of the fighting!

"And every day I came and brought them a meal in a basket—because, after all, they have to eat, right?

"And I walked through all the Red Guard soldiers—Where are you going, you beauty?—I'm bringing food to my sick mother; I left her behind on the other side of the Moscow River. 'We know what this sick mother looks like! She has a mustache and a beard!' Oh no, I don't like mustachioed or bearded men: the mustachioed one is a cat—and the bearded one is a goat! It's true I am going to see my mother! (I was already crying.)

"(He said:) 'Well, if it's true—go on to mama, go ahead, you can come back through, but just keep an eye out. Otherwise, if it's your time—someone might kill you, either one of us or them—and your old mother will be left without any lunch.'"

I always looked at the Cathedral of Christ the Savior with a lot of feeling, because I used to bring meals to them, to my darlings.

"Marina! You know, I can be a terrible liar sometimes! And I believe them myself. Yesterday, I was standing in line, I got into a conversation with a soldier—a kind one; he was waiting for the same thing. First we talked about prices. Then—more important, more *sery-ious* (her pronunciation) things. What a nice young lady you are, young, smart. You know everything, you know the truth about everything. Yes, but I'm not a young lady at all! And my husband is with Kolchak![XVII] And I say it over and over, and I cry a lot—I say I love him so much and fear for him—because I know that he will not reach Moscow—because I don't really have a husband who is advancing with Kolchak . . ."

***

Sonechka adored my children: six-year-old Alya and two-year-old Irina. The first thing she did when she came over was take Irina out of her crib.

"How's my little girl? Did you recognize your Gollidey? How do you sing about me? Golly-da, Golly-da! dey-dey-dey! Right?"

Irina would be on her knees, Alya under Sonecka's right arm—the one not occupied with Irina. ("I always carry children on my left side, don't you? To protect them with my right. And to hug them.") And so there were the three of them: a group of three heads frozen in still life bliss; Irina with her high forehead, I almost said with horns, with her large sheep-like bright golden curls above her protruding forehead, then Alya, pale-golden, doll-like, head like a knight's cupola, and between them Sonechka, with her smooth curly, brown chestnut hair, petrified in the bliss of their perfect embrace, her head dipping—from one to the other. And what's funny—the adult Sonechka was only slightly bigger than the children:

> Mother who bore you
> Was an early rose:
> A petal, she dropped—
> The moment you were born . . . [Balmont]

(Only when I recall Sonechka do I comprehend these comparisons of women to flowers, and eyes to stars, lips to petals, and so on—until the dawn of time.

It's not that I comprehend them, but she inspires me to create these images.)

***

They stayed with me like that—as a group. They were like a photograph.

***

When Irina slept, Sonechka would sit with Alya on her lap. It was a perfect vision of Florence with her brother Dombey: Dickens would have died seeing them together!

***

Sonechka with my children was the perfect vision of motherhood—virginal motherhood, maternal virginity: not girlfriends, but girl Virgin Marys:

Before their firstborn—Virgin Marys
That's right, no you can't translate it!

"Well, now enough about Galli-da, if not I'll get too vain! Now sing 'Ay doo-doo' (for Alya and me, in a low voice—it's the same thing!)— well, how do you sing it?

Ay doo doo
Ay doo doo
The soldier sits on the oak tree
He plays his *t'umpet*
His *t'umpet*
His *t'umpet*

"Yes, yes, my dear! Only there is more: 'The trumpet is so fine and gold-plated'—but that might be difficult for you. When you are older then."

And so on—for hours, never getting tired, never getting bored, never fading.

"Marina, I will never have children."

"Why?"

"I don't know. The doctor told me and explained it to me, but all the internal body stuff is so complicated for me . . ."

She was serious, like a grown woman, with eyelashes already fluttering like the edges of stars.

There was no greater grief for her than to come to my children empty-handed.

"I don't have anything, absolutely nothing today, my little one!" she'd say to Irina's questioning eyes. "You see, I waited until the last minute—I kept hoping that they would give out things . . . But they didn't—because they are awful—they killed the Tsar, and they left my Irina without food . . . But I promise you, really, I promise: next time, in addition, I will bring you some sugar . . ."

"Sugee, gimme!" said Irina—joyfully insistent.

"Irina, how can you say that!" Alya, out of embarrassment, was ready to cover Irina's mouth with her hand.

And Sonechka's explanation meant nothing to Irina except for the word *sugar*—sugar would be tomorrow. But tomorrow is also when Irina would go to bed, and then she'd wake up, and her mother would wash her face and hands, and give her some potatoes, and . . .

"Gimme po-tay-toes!"

"Oh, my dear little one, I don't even have any potatoes today, I'm talking about tomorrow . . ." said Sonechka, with sincere embarrassment.

"Sonechka!" said Alya, worriedly. "You can't talk about food with Irina, because she understands it all very well—it's the only thing she understands—and now she won't stop asking for it!

"Oh, Marina! How sad it was to know I would never have children. But now, it seems, I'm happy about it. It's horrible, so horrible—I would simply go crazy if my child were asking for food and I had nothing to give her . . . However, there are all the other people's children . . ."

There weren't any strangers for her. Neither children, nor people.

***

Two entries from Alya's notebook in the spring of 1919 (six years old):

Evening came, I started to wash myself. Suddenly, a knock on the door. With my face still wet, I threw Marina's silk shawl over me and quickly went downstairs and asked: Who's there? (Marina knew a girl-like actress Sofia Evgenievna Gollidey.) From behind the door, I heard:

"It's me, Alya, it's Sonya!" I quickly opened the door and said:

"Sofia Evgenievna!"

"Darling! My dearest child! My little one!" exclaimed Gollidey, but I quickly went up the stairs to Marina and said enthusiastically:

"Gollidey!"

But Marina was not there, because she had gone up to the attic with Yura N.

I start washing my feet. Suddenly, I heard a knock at the kitchen door. I opened it. Sofia Evgenievna entered. She sat down on a chair, put me on her lap and said: "They abandoned you, my poor sweet child! I'm thinking we need to invite all the guests here."

"What do you mean? I want to wash my feet."

"Oh, yes, that's no good."

I put my face on Gollidey's soft shoulder. Gollidey was barely touching my shawl. She left, promising to come back to say goodbye. But when she didn't come back, I went around wearing just a shirt and throwing a shawl over my shoulders. Then I went over to Gollidey and sat on her knees. Yura S., another student from the Studio, was there, and Gollidey. Marina had gone with Yura N. up to the attic a little earlier. I arrived without shoes or sandals—only my black stockings. It was so sweet! Yura S. gave me a small pie. Gollidey was cheerful and stroked my tangled hair.

Then Gollidey's friend came, and we heard footsteps on the roof. It turned out that Marina and Yura N. had gone together to the roof through the attic window. Yura S. climbed onto the roof with a candle and shouted: "Give me some light here so I can save the mistress of the house!" I was sitting on the windowsill, moving closer to the roof. Gollidey was calling out to her friend and saying: "Oh dear, the child is going out to the roof! Get that foolish child!"

A young lady came up to get me, but I struggled. Finally, Gollidey herself got me down from the window to put me to bed. I didn't struggle but I said: "Gollidey is ugly! I don't like Gollidey!" She smiled and gave me to Yura S., saying I was too heavy for her. They had just sat me down when suddenly I saw Marina coming down from the attic. (While Gollidey was carrying me, she kept saying: "Alya, calm down! You will be the first to see Marina!") Marina was holding a large candle in a copper candleholder in her hands. Gollidey told Marina: Marina, Alechka said that she doesn't love me anymore!

Marina was very surprised, I think.

The actress Sonechka came to our house. We were sitting in the kitchen. It was dark. She said to me: "You know, Alechka, Yura wrote me this note: Dear little Sonechka! I'm very glad you don't love me. I'm a very nasty person. You mustn't like me. Don't like me. But I thought he wrote this on purpose so that people would love him even more. And not despise him. I didn't say anything to him."

Sonechka Gollidey had a small pink face and dark eyes. She was short, with thin arms. I kept thinking about him and said to myself: He calls out to this woman so she will love him. He writes her little notes on purpose. If he thought he was being a nasty person, he wouldn't have written this.

***

. . . Not nasty. Only weak. Passionless. No passion except for ambition—so generously and unfortunately fed by her beauty. What do I remember from his statements? To each of my edgy, point-blank questions about preferences, choosing this or that—even between the Reds and the Whites he'd say: I don't know what . . . It's all so complicated . . . (And also: "it's far from simple in reality." Or, "It's all the same to me"). He was only excited by the theater, I remember him telling me once, for over an hour, about how he would love to make (with his own hands?) a small theater and divide it into countless cells. Each cell would have little men, characters from their own plays and from the play common to all the cells . . . What would this be exactly, these plays . . . What would be the point? He'd say mysteriously: "I don't know . . . I don't really know yet. But I have a vision . . . (blissfully)—They'd be so small you could hardly see them . . .

Sometimes—he had vague dreams of Italy: "When we leave, Pavlik and I will go to Italy . . . we will walk through the hills of Florence, eat salty braided bread, drink Chianti, and pick tangerines from a tree . . ." I'd say, echoing: "And evoke—Marina . . ." (He echoes my echo:) "And evoke—Marina . . ."

But his Italy was also Goldoni's—and not the depths of melancholy.

One day Pavlik said to me: "Marina? Yura has decided to stage Shakespeare." (Me, amused:) "And?"

"Yes. Macbeth. And you know what—he won't even keep half of it!"

"He'd better add in the other half. Make an effort. Did Shakespeare forget something? And Yuri Alexandrovich figured it out and filled it in?"

Once, after his ramblings and delusions of fame—after all, he'd grown up in the volcanic delusions of the theatrical-to-the-bone Vakhtangov—I said to him: "Yuri Alexandrovich, for once in your life listen to the truth. Women love you, and you want men to esteem you."

His fellow students—except for Pavlik, who was in love with him, like Pushkin was in love with Goncharova—were an exception. But Pavlik (the fact that Goncharova was a woman, and Yuri Alexandrovich Zavadsky was a man, changed nothing at all, for even Pushkin by marrying Goncharova did not take on her beauty; he stayed small and wiry, etc.)—Pavlik's love also had to overcome jealousy: his decision to love—when in reality he should have hated, but Pavlik's love was purely romantic—and so, except for Pavlik, his comrades at the Studio related to him in a condescending way—as opposed to us who loved him, also in a condescending way, condescending to our weakness, and subject to his seductions.—"Zavadsky . . . ye-ah . . ."—but this drawn-out *yes* was not followed by anything else.

(The love between Yuri and Pavlik was a mutual jealousy: Yuri—for talent; Pavlik—for beauty. The jealousy was so unbearable that it turned into—love. And there was also a secret calculation that fell into place: together they added up to—Lord Byron.)

Yuri was an emanation of his own beauty. But since his focus (beauty) was naturally strong, his other qualities were insufficient, and so he was unworthy of her. Still, it's a tragedy for a man when his face is the best thing about him and beauty is so primary—when his face is what sells, and the face itself becomes a product.

Everyone was making demands on him because of his beauty: the directors and the women. Everyone was going around begging. (I alone gave him credit for his beauty.) "But, still, gentlemen, I never promised anything special to anyone . . ."

"No, my friend, such a face already is a promise. Only don't promise something you can't keep. Flowers can keep such promises. And precious stones. Precious through and through. Floral through and through. Or saints like Saint Sebastian. It must be said that he wore his beauty humbly, like an angel. (Where do I get this from?) But this did not improve things, it only worsened the matter. The only way out for a man is not to condescend to his beauty, but to despise it (the meaning of despise is to look down on). But for this, you need to be a better person. He was a lesser person, he deluded himself just like the rest of us . . .

How to describe the Angel? An angel does not consist of parts, but a unified piece. He makes himself known. He waits. When we speak of an angel, there can be no doubt: we all see an angel the same way.

Let me add: with a white streak. Twenty years—and white lock of hair, a pure silver streak.

And also—a fur coat with a beaver collar. A huge fur coat, because his height was superhuman: the height of an angel.

Apart from this superhuman size, he had no substance, no shape, no "figure." He himself was the figure.

The year 1919 favored his angelness: whether it was the endlessness of his fur coat or the cloak of St. Anthony—that is, always his clothes and always—a haziness. Due to this, he didn't really have a face: only the outward dips and drifts, "from one meadow to another—the whimsical wind blowing—chasing golden reflections" (silver ones).

He had the classic face of an angel, so unmistakably that any young girl would have recognized him in a dream. And she did.

But his angelic appearance was somewhat superficial, yet there certainly *was* truly something of an angel in him: his voice (the most internal of our inner parts, and the French say *organ*), his cautious gestures, how he bowed his head to listen, or how he'd place his two palms under while raising his head. His way of suddenly appearing—a motionless vision in the doorway—or of disappearing without a trace.

His beauty, the angelic essence of his beauty, taught him something, showed him something, dictated his steps ("he steps so carefully, as if he's afraid to crush some tiny invisible creatures," said Alya), and his gestures and intonation. But he couldn't say anything meaningful with words. She could not teach him anything about intelligence—it was not his business to be intelligent—that is why he could not *say* anything well (there was nothing to say!); he could only give an impression—that's all.

And so everyone was deceived: from the simplest cleaning lady to Sonechka and me. "He loves so much he can't even speak . . ." (*So*—it meant he didn't love, didn't love at all.) "A kind of mystery . . ." There was no mystery. None—except the mystery itself of such beauty.

Beauty can (and does!) teach you to *step forward*, to *perform*—to *act*, no, to show off, maybe—to say something smart? No, it was all about the right voice, the right intonation, the right place to pause, the breath. But the right words—no. Here we enter a different realm, where we are the princes, Infanta's dwarfs.

It wasn't that "he was a kind of angel," but everything about him was angelic—except his words and his gait, his words and actions. These were most ordinary, those of a schoolboy and an actor—the best of his age and circle, at least not the worst. They were only *ordinary* against the backdrop of such beauty.

When I say, in a way, he was faceless, it was a persona—not a mask. Yes—an appearance. An angelic look on an ordinary (uninhabited) building. An image, an impression (what I am now writing—an epitaph), but, anyway, it's better to have it—than not!

For *him*—it was all in the past. It's been almost twenty years! His age at that time! And my poetic outpouring, in my poem "The Comedian,"—for him, about him, addressed to him at that time, my play *Lauzun* (Fortune)—with his actual voice in the room, in the freezing cold, under a dark blue sky, and an eighteenth-century lantern:

Is it possible—these hands
Of mine—are cracking
My hands, what a pity!
The devil take this frost!

(This "devil" sounded more tender than a lute!)—I see the play of midnight-blue light and light blue shadow on his frightened, watchful hand . . . *For him.* I wrote my play (now lost) *The Stone Angel* dedicated to Sonechka Gollidey. It's about a stone angel in a village square, where brides abandon grooms, wives abandon husbands, absolute love for love: the reason one throws oneself in the water to drown, poisons themselves, is cloistered—yet the angel just stands there . . . No further action necessary.

Well and good that my notebook disappeared—similarly drowned, poisoned, cloistered—the same way . . . *His* shadow is projected in my poems to Sonechka (and all over them!). But *him*—it's another story. What has been said is only to understand Sonechka better, to show what they were attached to, what they were inextricably drawn to, in that spring of 1919, what they were filled to the brim with and why her huge, chestnut-colored eyes always sparkled.

Sonechka! Let's forgive her angelic resemblance.

***

One day I went to see him, bringing another gift. I didn't find him—I found the nanny.

"A book for Yuri? Thank you. Let him read it and amuse himself. So few of them come with something, my dear—you're sweet to bring him a gift. A lot come to see him. Morning till night they come. As soon as he opens his eyes—they call, and when he closes his eyes—they call again. And more and more come, empty-handed too, and kiss-kiss.

"Yes, I don't blame those ladies—they are so young! Yurochka is good, good-looking, he was always so good. He was born like that. He's good—I still feel him in my arms. All the young ladies fall in love with him, I even said to him: Why are you, Yuri Alexandrovich, so good? This is not right for a man—to be so good!

'Yes, nanny, but I'm not to blame.' Course not, but it's not easy for me to open doors all the time then run away . . . Let them kiss you! (they won't stop anyway.) Only: if you kiss them, then make sure that you get some rice, millet, or just flatbread—don't you see how skinny he is.

"His sister, Verochka, has been suffering from tuberculosis a year already, it's not right, and him—they're the same face, same blood. But not him, of course, he's shy, he won't take anything. And to me in the kitchen he says: 'Here, nanny, help your beloved one.' But where are you going? He comes to my kitchen—of course I love him—and cries. Head empty, hands empty. But his mouth is open: full of stupid things and kisses.

"But she comes alone to him—golden. (Two more come around, one of them is kind of strict, like a governess, and her nose is too big, so let's not talk about them now . . .) You know that young lady Gollidey? She comes in and says: 'Is Yura home?' First she says Yuri Alexandrovich, but then quickly turns around and is not shy with me no more.

"He's home, I say, the beautiful one, only he's sleeping. She says, 'well, don't awake him up then, don't awake him, I won't even come inside, I just brought this for him, but, nanny, don't tell him . . .

"And she pops open her bag, and in the bag there's not much millet or rye bread, but always a *bulochka* [sweet bun]: A *bulochka* . . . Where on earth does she find them?!

"Or she sits down and darns his socks: Give me Yura's socks, Nanny."

"What are you saying, My Lady, what are you doing with your young hands? This is old woman's work."

"'No way!' and she is so warm, so warm, and she looks tender, tenderly into my eyes and says, 'Don't call me My Lady, call me Sonya, and I'll call you Nanny.'

"So I began calling her Sonechka, like a little cutie.

"Well, she really loves him—I can say that! She mends his socks, irons his shirt (but our guy is still asleep, doesn't know anything), she kisses me on the cheek and says—'And Nanny, give my greetings to Yurochka'—and runs off.

"How many times did I say to my handsome guy: Don't think too much, Yuri Alexandrovich, you won't find anyone better anywhere: she's beautiful and smart and hardworking, and she acts in the theater—she supports herself. On a dark night she can run to the doctor—bring the whole city to their feet and can even bring over a doctor. With such a wife you can be sick! She'd be a good mother to your children, since she chose you, such a big oaf, as a son. If she just would grow a little more: he's, you know—like so enormous and she, well, what a little thing she is! (To me she says: 'Big guys always love little ones.') A gold coin may be so small—but so precious."

"And what does he do?"

"Stands, smiles, stays silent. Doesn't like it—that's what."

"Does he love someone else?"

"Eh, my sweetheart, he doesn't love anyone, he never loved anyone, 'cept Verochka's sisters, and me, his Nanny." (I, to myself: And himself in the mirror.)

"So about Sonechka, just to finish off. If she doesn't find him home, she leaves cheerfully, but if she finds him, she always bursts into tears. But he's cold."

"He's a cold one with you."

The mirror is cold too.

***

Sonechka had her own nanny—Maryushka. "I will get married—with a yellow chest—as a dowry." Not a nanny—she was an old servant, but an old servant caregiver, yet still—a nanny.

During my entire friendship with Sonechka, I never saw this Maryushka—because she was always standing in line: for *vobla*, [dry fish] for vegetable oil, or for something else. But I constantly heard about her, over and over, "Maryushka will be angry again" (about Yura and the sleepless nights and the handfuls of millet . . .)

One day there was a knock on the door. I opened it. Her eyes were dark and took over her face.

She exclaimed: "Marina! A terrible thing happened. A coffin moved into my room."

"Wha-a-at?"

"Listen. My Maryushka heard they were giving out coffins—yes—real coffins (a pause)—well, you know, for the dead—because now it's a luxury, you know what they did for Alexey Alexandrovich at the Studio—they've already given out all of them, so they won't give us one. She went—and took care of him every day she went there—until finally the clerk lost patience.

"'Maybe you'll die soon, grandma, and you won't be hanging around here all the time waiting for a coffin? Grandma, you'll die before we get you a coffin'—and other pleasantries, but she was firm: 'I was promised— really I was promised, and I won't back down.' She kept going and going, and finally she went and there it was! Yes, yes, with the number 30 from the ration card.

"'Well, you finally got it, old lady, you got what you wanted?' And he places it in the middle of the bench—a blue one—'Well, go ahead and measure it, will you fit in it with all your little bones?'

"'I'll fit, I'll fit, but never in that one.'

"'What do you mean—not in that one?'

"'Cause, I mean, that one—is a blue one, it's a man's one—but I'm a maiden, I need a pink one. Be so kind and give me a little pink one—cause no way can I have a blue one.'

"'Wha-a-at?' he says, 'listen, old hag, you're making my blood boil, and what's more, now you're some kind of *maiden girl*, you want to lay down in a pink one! You won't have any pink ones, damn it, because we don't have any in our factory.'

"'Okay well then give me a little white one, your lordship,'—I said to him, and I got scared to death, thinking I would end up going without a coffin—because, you know, for a girl to lie in a man's blue thing is a dishonor, and all my life I've been honest from baby swaddling clothes to the shroud. Suddenly he stomped on me with his feet: 'You damn girl, take what you can get—and get out of here, otherwise I'll give you trouble!' He was yelling about the Revolution, a big commotion going on. They can't even tell the difference anymore—the men from the women, especially the dead ones . . .

"'Take it, take it, I say, or I'll kill you with that very thing!' And then he started swinging at me—with that coffin lid! Shame, fear, and the soldiers standing around—cackling and pointing fingers . . .

"Well, I saw there's nothing left to do, I took with me my eternal resting place and went away, and so, my Lady, I'm bitterly sad, how much I hung around waiting, how much ridicule I endured. Now I'll have to rest in a man's blue one.

"And now, Marina, it's in my room. You know that very deep shelf above the door—for suitcases? She begged me to get it off the floor and out of sight, and most importantly, not to bother her eyes: the color.

"Because soon as I look at it, my lady, I'm filled with spite.

"It's worth it, though? (Pause.)—I'll probably get used to it—someday, anyway!"

***

(It was the feast of the Ascension 1919.)

***

The *fourth* character in Sonechka's room was the coffin.

***

But here my Sonechka was seen through different eyes: those of strangers.

"I saw your Sonechka Gollidey today. I was riding the tram and saw her standing, holding a leather loop, reading something, smiling. And suddenly a huge soldier's gigantic paw landed on her shoulder. And do you know what she did? While holding onto the leather loop and reading, even while smiling, she calmly took his paw off her shoulder—like it was a thing."

"That's her—the one and only! Are you sure it was her?"

"Oh yeah. I saw her many times in *White Nights*, it was her, the very same one, in a white dress, with two braids. It was so . . . Purr-fect (my interlocutor's accent was from the Kingdom of Poland) that the whole tram car burst out laughing and one guy even shouted: Bravo!"

"And what did she say?"

"Nothing. And she didn't even look up. Maybe she smiled a little more . . . She's really very pretty."

"You think so?"

"With her drooping eyelids and those braids, she's a real prima donna. She probably has a lot of love affairs?"

"No. She only loves little children . . ."

"But, that doesn't . . ."

"Yes, it's a shame."

***

That's how I kept Sonechka from the clutches—of bourgeois paws.

Did she have romances?

I never knew exactly what her relationships were with men, whether they were so-called affairs—or other kinds of relationships. But dreaming together or sleeping together, in the end, always meant crying alone.

Part Two
Volodya

The first impression of him as a human being is his stature. Immediately striking is his stance: a triangle turned on its head, where the shoulders are everything and the waist is down to nothing.

The first impression produced by his face is the letter T with the cross at the top: a vertical wrinkle, connecting the eyebrows and continuing down the straight line of his nose.

But here—we must pause, for all the other visual impressions are secondary.

A deep voice, resounding from his deepest depths and therefore resonating in the depths. It was breathtakingly deep and deeply breathtaking.

But not musical in the least. Nothing like an instrument, it was very human, to the full extent of his humanity and his vocal cords.

"There's a man!" From head to toe.

Even his youth yielded to his image of manliness—this *homme*. Only afterwards one learned he was actually young—very young indeed. Think of Hugo's couplet:[1] if you replaced his youth with the Consul, and his adult man self with the Emperor—there's Volodya:

After being the First Consul, already, in many places
The Emperor's forehead broke through the narrow mask

The man within him manifested himself before our eyes everywhere. He was ubiquitous.

This very young man actually bore the face of his future older self.

For a whole year now, I'd been hearing about Volodya A. and each time from Pavlik A.—with his steadfast exclamation—extraordinary. "There is an extraordinary man in our Studio—Volodya A." At this time he did not bring *this* particular friend to me.

Our first meeting was in winter of 1918-1919, on the icy descent of 1918, at the home of a most merry and young-looking woman, who skillfully raised up her leg and arm simultaneously, and this leg-arm raising was a greeting for the arts—for me and my poetry among them. There were many women of this kind from the old world, celebrating the end of their youth during the Revolution[II] at its beginning. But by 1919 they were all gone.

The first words from that deep voice were: "But kings not only succumbed to traditions—they create them."

They were his first words to me, at the end of the evening. We did not say a word to each other otherwise (he was sitting watching the card game, I was not):

"You remind me of Georges Sand—she also had children—and she *also* wrote—and she also had a hard life—on Majorca, in times when the stoves were not used for heat."

I invited him over immediately. He came the next morning—we went walking around. He was hungry. I shared my piece of bread with him as we sat outside.

Then he said: "I really liked you immediately, everything about you right away. And that you invited me over right away, not even knowing me. And you yourself suggested tomorrow. Women never do that; it's always the day after tomorrow, as if they knew they were very busy the next day. And we did not sit at home, but went out. And we split the bread in half, and ate it together. I sensed in all this a ritual."

And then, much later he said: "You know when we were at Zoya Borisovna's, you reminded me of a Polish noble lady. You were wearing some kind of long jacket (unable to find the word) with long sleeves and a sash? Smoke-colored, velvety, with a trim. Like an old-fashioned Polish caftan. And the incline of your head—a bit back. And your eyes a bit upwards. Immediately I sensed in you Polish blood."

He began to come over regularly. He came over often—once or twice a week, right after a performance, that is, after midnight. We'd sit at opposite ends of the burnt-orange sofa just like this: he'd be deep in one corner, while I, slightly askew on its outer edge on the other end. The conversation proceeded along a diagonal line, the longest path from one end to the other.

Eyes quite big and dark but seemingly dark because of his eyelashes, while they themselves were grey. His whole face was straight, not a curve, without the slightest wrinkle, as if carved with a chisel. His face had the same sort of linearity as in a silhouette: the head of his body. His stance was just like his face. The only thing that was not straight in this whole picture was his hair parted to the side, which in itself was straighter than if it had been in the middle.

Outwardly straight, internally straight. Voice, movement, eye-expression, handshake. All one direction and following the shortest line between the two points: him and the world.

Linear and rigid. Inflexible. Despite complete openness, he was absolutely impregnable. Not in the sense of being enigmatic or mysterious, but in the simplest sense: what he was made of was impenetrable. This was a person you could not touch—and if you did touch him, you wouldn't reach anything but a hand, you wouldn't disturb a thing. Therefore, it was useless to touch. Absolutely, it's as if he were a statue, palpable, reachable, but impenetrable. In a way, something without any depth.

In a word, despite its physical nonexistence or maybe because of it, he was the furthest he could be from a portrait. Infinitely reachable and willing, yet at will, you could *look* deep into a frame of the soul or extract from the depths of centuries to bring it into the room. The very opposite of a portrait, that is—a statue, which, by its extreme obviousness and manifestation, limits the gaze at every point of its surface.

(Is this really me—Marina Ivanovna? Yes, it's all you, Volodechka. But, it's too soon to be upset about it—wait.)

(How did it become clear later that the impression of his statuesqueness was wrong? And I fed on this mistake for a year and a half, a year and a half I built it up—and created it.)

He became my friend immediately. A true friend—a pillar.

In Moscow of 1918-1919, what was courageous, upright and strong like steel in me, I could not share with anyone, really. In Moscow of 1918-1919, among the youth of my circle was, let's be truthful—there were only scoundrels left. A number of "Studio Members" at the theater were taking refuge from the war and finding shelter in the newly opened studios with their talent. And there was the Red Youth[III], who took shelter between battles, possibly wonderful but with whom I could not be friends, for there could be no friendship between the defeated and the victors.

With Volodya I could pour out my male spirit.

I immediately started calling him Volodechka with the greatest gratitude that he was not in love, nor was I, and everything was very relaxed and going well.

He called me Marina Ivanovna, he could not give up my patronymic,[IV] and we always said goodbye by name and patronymic. I was even thankful for that—in those days everyone was calling me Marina. It's just that no one else called me Marina Ivanovna! He said goodbye with my patronymic, he immediately was different from the others, bestowing on me my patronymic and in his own way he made me his own.

Our conversations? They were about the stars; one time returning home from visiting someone, we stood for an hour in my alley, knee-deep in snow. I remember his raised hand, going higher and higher—and the name Flammarion [French astronomer]—the *Flammarions* of his eyes, only looking into mine, so that my eyes would look up to the stars. The snowdrift grew and grew: there was no storm—only stars, but the snowdrift stood so long it kept growing—or did we grow into it?—we could have stood there another hour—and a house of ice would have taken shape, and we'd be in it.

And what else? Joan of Arc—the miracle of her appearance—we'd talk about Napoleon at St. Helene's, about Jack London, his favorite writer at the time, but never about the theater.

And not about poetry either. I never went on about poetry to him. Didn't talk about it, nor write any poems for him. We had a deeper love, deeper than poetry. More necessary to both of us. As it should be—more necessary than he was to me or I to him.

I knew nothing about his life (his love affairs, his family). And I never asked. He came out of the depths of that winter night and went into a darker night after hours of being there—then left. ("Already the light . . ."—it would come later.)

And I consciously did not walk him out. Volodya ended and began at the threshold. The interval was his life.

I swear, I do not remember making any kind of arrangements . . . like when he would come over, etc. But there was never a time—all winter, that he'd come and not find me at home, and never a time when there were other people with me. We didn't have "days" either, sometimes twice a week or once every two.

"You mean you were always home and always alone?" No, I'd go out. People would come over. But it was our very own magic, and every single time I would see him and cry out: "Volodya, I was just thinking about you!" Or "Volodya, if you only knew how much I wished you would come today!" Or simply: "Volodya, what luck!"

Because along with him came happiness—for the entire evening, really and truly—like a favorite book that you don't need any light to read.

Happiness without any fears about the next day: Would he suddenly stop loving me? What if he did not come over anymore? And so forth. And no tomorrow? What about expecting him and his long strides walking through the streets, and standing around with feet freezing—and nights freezing—at the window?

Can I say any more: I never yearned for Volodya, as surely as I never missed him. I was always happy to see him. I dreamed of him—in a peaceful way, as one dreams about things one will always have, like a registered letter one knows will come. (Its arrival is the post office's problem, not mine.)

At my house, he'd always take off his fur coat. Whether there was cold or frost—he always took off his fur coat. In a gray, elegant, fitted suit, just as distinguished as he himself was, his figure was totally contoured—separate from the objects and walls surrounding him. He remained seated, not leaning on anything, and if he leaned he never slouched, as if behind his back was not a wall but a big rock. The view behind him was definitely the sea. When I saw him later on stage (only one time this happened!), it was a play with a marine theme—either *The Shipwreck of Hope* or *The Deluge*—I never felt a separation from my Volodya, on the contrary—perhaps for the first time it was then I saw him in his true nature: marine and male.

***

For over a year now, I heard Pavlik say "Volodya is gorgeous—not like Yura, of course, that is to say, just as handsome but not the same . . . you know what I mean? Yura could easily have been a beauty, while Volodya no way . . ."

That's why I took Volodya's beauty for granted when I saw him and never thought about it again. I mean, I treated it as if he was born with it, like a given. It didn't bother him or fill him with confusion, or me either. His beauty did not stand between us—it wasn't like a persistent child, who always needed attention or comfort, otherwise he'd set fire to the house.

I want to say from the very beginning there was nothing else between us. There was only our long-talks-on-the-sofa path to each other, from one end to the other. There was one person (me) before this perfect statue of a man. Maybe I sat further away from him in order to see him better—to give the statue the possibility of being viewed better, creating a perspective which I was deprived of in his presence. And through this perspective that I physically created, replacing the one which some people call the future, and what a man and a woman would call love.

One day I jokingly asked him: "Volodechka, do women bother you when they talk about your beauty? Do they cling to you?"

He smiled shyly but said frankly: "Marina Ivanovna, they cling to the young guys, especially the actors. Afraid of a wolf . . . I feel sorry for all the women. Especially the not so young ones. Because we are all terribly guilty before them. Guilty of everything."

"What about you?"

"Me?" he says sincerely. "I try to make amends."

Besides me, he was friends with a woman in the Studio—her last name was Caucasian. When he talked about her a lot, I jokingly got jealous and made fun of her a bit, without having seen her. But he kept saying: "No, no, Marina Ivanovna, you can't laugh at her, even jokingly. Because she is a wonderful person."

Unyielding, like a rock.

"She nursed the wounded during the war—and received the highest recognition."

"Well, I did not."

"You—no, you had something else to do."

"You mean sitting and writing poetry. You know I'm offended!"

"No, not sitting and writing poetry—but doing what you do."

"And what do I do?"

"What you do with me and what you will always do with me."

"Volodya, come on!"

"*Come on.*"

One day he brought her to me. And oh, my goodness! The young lady turned out to not be pretty. Really, not pretty. Obviously, not as pretty as he was handsome. He preferred this plain homely one to someone else he was with when he was not with me, and let himself be spoiled and loved by her.

Was that his attempt to make amends?

***

Volodya came to me with the gift of his stories, as if brought in the palms of his hands—so concrete, they were brought physically to my own house—and he placed them in my heart, as if it was putting them into own hands.

I remember one story of his about a French pilot killed during the war—his aircraft broken, the man killed. After some time, the victorious bird returns and descends, and tramples enemy land. A victorious German presents a wreath to the downed Frenchman.

Those stories nourished me during those long, long nights.

None of them about the theater, only once did he laugh and say: "Marina Ivanovna, you're not suspicious of me, are you? Of being overly ambitious? I am not really so vain."

"No."

"Because it's been said before, and you would appreciate it. We have a cleaning lady in the Studio, she's sweet, young, and everyone teases her that she's in love with me. It's nonsense, of course, but I joke with her and chat with her—she's young, and she could easily be my partner and not a cleaning lady. For women, birth and class play a much smaller role than for men. Women have only two categories: youth and old age. Right? She was just telling me today. After I removed my makeup and was wiping my face: 'Oh, Volodechka Alexeyev, what a cruelly handsome man you are!' 'What do you mean, Dunya, handsome? Isn't Zavadsky the one with cruel beauty?' 'No,' she said, 'Yuri (Alexandrovich) is angelic, an urban kind of handsome, while you, Volodechka, have a military, truly irresistible, virile beauty of a hero. In the countryside, Yuri Alexandrovich would be a laughingstock, but you, Volodechka, three entire villages would have already gone crazy over you.'

He says thoughtfully: "So that's the kind of hero I am."

"Beauty can be frightening . . ."[V] And now, Volodya, to rhyme with your austere beauty, I will tell you my story:

From childhood I remember Marya Vasilievna at our house—I don't know why, but she did everything. If one of the children got sick, she took care of him; if the trunks needed cleaning, she'd empty them out; if there was sewing or dyeing of eggs to do, it was her. Then she disappeared. She got thin—almost a skeleton, but truly magnificent eyes, so mournful, really mournful eyes: dark brown, (not black, only eyes further east are black—or those who are very stupid—beady) as big as her face that was not there. Although she was old, she was not really an old woman—not a single white hair, black almost blue, parted in the middle. Well, even better, a nun—like the older Mother Mary bent over her son. Yes, that's how it was—I was still little then—she had a son, Sasha, at the modern high school, he lived in our addition, near the kitchen. Then my mother and I went abroad and he fell ill with tuberculosis. My father sent him to Sukhumi.

"Oh, Musenka, how he waited for me, how he longed for me! Every ship that came in. When he heard the steamboat blow its whistle: 'It's my mother coming finally. She's coming to see me!' (The nurse told me later.) And I actually did go—your dad gave me some money, and the janitor at the station bought me a ticket and put me on the train—it was the first time I had traveled so far. I arrived, and he was waiting for me. And just as we were about to dock, the steamer sounded its horn. He sat up in bed, stretched out his arms: Mother has arrived!—and fell down dead . . ."

I want to put a face to her name, because she had that same face even when she was cooking semolina porridge or telling stories about the pug belonging to the general's wife's—always with the same face. But now—about that cruel beauty—here's a story from her young days:

"Musenka, don't look at me, I'm wrinkled as a mummy and yellower than a lemon with loose teeth. But, Musenka, when I was young I used to be a beauty. I was fifteen then. I went to a shop for some reason and a young man came in behind me. I went out and he followed me. I entered the house, looked out of the window—he was standing there, looking at my curtains. He was a dark-haired man, and such eyes—oh, a mustache, not even starting to grow yet. Well, he was about sixteen years old or something. And, I swear, he looked like me—my ears were ringing from hearing them talked about, my eyes, my face. But really his eyes were mine, yes they were. Well, in a word—he was my brother. (I grew up an only child.) Only—it's a long story, but it's quickly over, and *hop!* I quickly closed the curtains.

"The next day—back to the shop, and he was already standing there, waiting. He didn't say anything, didn't bow, just looked. It all started like this: he followed me like a shadow and stood—like a stump. On the fifth day, or something like that, my heart couldn't stand it: it annoyed me the way he looked at me, and annoyed me the way he was silent. As soon as I left, he came out after me. I told him, 'There's nothing to see, no reason to stand there, because you won't see anything, I'm engaged: I'm marrying a rich person.'

"It was spring, he stood under the sweet trees, taking off his cap, and bowing down really low. And he turned white as a sheet. The next day—while I was still sleeping—there was a scream, a loud noise: at the Egorovs, a little one had cut his throat during the night. It happened during the night, I think, because he's completely cold. Everyone ran there—and me too, I ran.

"And there he lay—Musenka—my recent acquaintance, the one who kept looking at me, only the eyes could no longer see: they were closed."

". . . Volodechka, what about your housekeeper?"

"No Marina Ivanovna, these are different times, now everything has lost its value. I would feel it if she loved me. No, she'll get married and have children."

"And she'll call the oldest one Volodechka."

"That *could* happen."

***

I nourished him with such stories during our long nights: with him in the far corner of the sofa at its edge, under a blue lamp, along the long diagonal, and I on its other edge—the embodiment of the long road that was to lead one to the other but by which we never got anywhere.

***

Now I think (and even then I knew!) that Volodya was a companion, and that the road was not leading to each other but—we each had our own road, only jointly—away from each other. Away from where we were, hence, the space and the serenity and reliability—and the absence of haste. One can only hasten to arrive at the eternal impasse, from which there is only one way out: backing out step by step and taking away everything that has been given, even trampling on things—to push them into the ground, and leveling everything, using one's foot like on a shovel.

***

I was bewitched—there is no other word for it. Volodya obviously knew I loved Yuri Zavadsky. But this didn't come up, and maybe it didn't concern him. Only when tormented by Yuri's long disappearances (he started disappearing, in fact, right away!) I began hearing a most indifferent voice say:

"How's Zavadsky? Is Zavadsky okay? Or is he fooling around?"

Zavadsky was the only subject of indulgence. When I said his name—he was immediately sent to a high tower, and me to the small garden below, in the pinkest of flowerbeds. And how good it felt for me to be diminished, feeling my grandeur and being equal to him—a little girl, forgetting herself and looking up at the stone angel from the pink kingdom below. For Volodya, I was always up in the tower, at the very top. in some way it was embarrassing to think of myself as that younger (and stupid) girl. It was even physically difficult for Yuri to raise his eyes when he spoke of him, and for me too—I spoke with lowered eyelids.

One day I burst out: "Volodya, do you despise me so much for . . ." But he was flabbergasted: "Me—despise you? Could I despise the sky above your head! Let's put an end to this once and for all: there are things that a man cannot understand about a woman. Even I, even about you. Not because it is below or above our understanding, that's not the point, but because some things can only be understood from the inside, *the internal.* I do not know what it is to be a woman. And so, that part of me that is masculine cannot understand that part of what is exclusively feminine in you. The one thousandth of myself is a thousandth that any woman would understand about you, even if that woman does not understand *anything* about you. Zavadsky—would be your common feminine secret (grinning)—even your conspiracy.

"I accept without question everything about you—and what you say—because for me you are beyond judgment."

"Is he a good actor?"

"His roles, yes, that is, where you don't need to act, just appear, be present, walk by, and speak. You see, I'm telling you honestly, I'm not overvaluing or undervaluing him. And it's not the actor in him that you . . ."

"Do you know, Volodechka, you who know everything—that I would give all of Zavadsky, all of my poems for him, all my feelings for him, in exchange for one hour of conversation with you—like now—you on one end and I on the other . . ."

Silence.

"What if I was given a choice—his entire self—or you with me—nothing but that? In a word, do you know that you take him from me with just a handshake. You take him away from my soul—as if he no longer existed?"

Still silent.

"But I am infinitely more than . . . ?!"

"I know, Marina Ivanovna."

***

Long, long days . . .

Not really, but:

Long, long nights . . .

When did he leave? Not at dawn, because in winter the day starts late, of course, but really at four in the morning? Or five? Where would he go? Where? (Without me.) Did he love someone like I loved Yuri Zavadsky? Was he healing from an unhappy, unworthy love like me? I don't know and never will.

***

I have never seen such a passion for justice in someone so young. (Not a passion for justice, but a passion for justice within him.) At the time he was twenty years old at most. "Why should I receive rations just because I am an actor and he is not? It's not fair." This was his main argument, the reason for his whole being, as if in reality (this was definitely reality!) justice had only one meaning, in all cases—indisputable, obvious, tangible, with its own weight, visible to the naked eye, from everywhere immediately visible and evident—like the golden dome of the Cathedral of Christ the Savior seen from the deepest corner of Neskuchny Garden.

If it was unfair, that was it. The thing no longer existed. There was no longer any temptation. Unfair—and it's a *no*. . . . This was not only in his head, it was in his backbone. Volodya A. held himself so straight because his backbone was justice itself.

Unjust—he declared it like Prince S. M. Volkonsky[VI] pronounced—it's ugly. Different generations, so a different vocabulary, but the same thing. Oh, how I recognize the compelling nature of this argument! A poor person would say: too expensive; or a merchant: impractical.

But Volodya would say: this is unjust.

His sense of injustice was justified.

***

Volodya, like all the studio members of his Studio, was a student of Stakhovich, but not in the same way as all the other studio members.

"M. I. Stakhovich taught us conclusions from all the centuries. The point was not to simply know how to greet a certain way but why you need to greet that way, how from the times of the savages we came to this greeting. For example, from tearing one another apart with one's teeth—to the idea of the duel. Stakhovich didn't teach us this (he smiles). We didn't have the time to learn the history of each gesture, we needed the gesture itself; the direct benefit and an immediate result: I'll go in and bow like Stakhovich; I'll go out fighting like Stakhovich—but I'll learn this on my own, going through his lessons in reverse—back to the source. And you know how difficult it is to find the origins of the Rhine or our race. For me, his bow and sophistication are not an answer but a question—a question posed by the past to the present. That's my question, and I, too, am trying to answer it, because, Marina Ivanovna (thoughtfully), I . . . I don't know . . . if Stakhovich himself would be able to answer it? These greetings were bestowed on Stakhovich from birth, a gift from his ancestors—when he was in his cradle. I have no ancestors, Marina Ivanovna, and no one put anything in my cradle. I came into the world naked, but even though I was naked, I shouldn't be senselessly dressing up in someone else's clothing, however superb. Their job was to bring them to me; mine was to imbue them with meaning.

"And I've already understood a lot, Marina Ivanovna, and I would say that it's far from being formulaic; on the contrary—it's foundational. Stakhovich taught us how *to be*. These are lessons for existence. Because—and forgive the crude example—

you can't bow like that and then punch each other. You can't even pronounce these words, or even think them, and if you can't think them—I'm already a different person, that bow is already inside me."

After Stakhovich's death, Volodya said to me: "I owe him a lot. At times I think—I'm young, Marina Ivanovna, and there's a Revolution going on. I'm often surrounded by crude people—I'm tempted to respond in kind, to use their language—a fist—and I immediately think: this was not—Stakhovich's way. And my tongue refuses to work. My arm does not lift. It will lift, Marina Ivanovna, at the right time—but never with a clenched fist!

At Stakhovich's funeral at the ruins of Devichye Polye:

Among the ruins of Devichye Polye
I advance behind the coffin swaying
Snowdrifts—potholes—snowdrifts
Moscow: the nineteenth century

. . . And among the other youth accompanying him, I remember Volodya especially. His erectness, his stance with the bumps and jolts, and above the snowdrifts—he never stepped away from his teacher, the way an eldest favorite grandson might have walked.

And what was it? What was that? Above the small shimmering crystal cross, astonishing in its purity and joy—two dark eyes, a rosy face, two black braids, as if she was embracing the cross—Sonechka was standing near the neighboring grave, it was Scriabin's[VII]. This was my first encounter with her since the *Blizzard* reading. Another snowstorm was roaring and raging over an open grave and the coffin could not fit into it: an aristocratic coffin, good quality, made at the Moscow Art Theater. The studio members sullenly made the grave bigger. They struck the frozen ground with their shovels, fought to the death with it, armed with spades that broke on the frozen earth. And a girl on her knees bent over the middle of a snowdrift, with her arms and braids wrapped around the crystal cross, flooded it with her tears, set ablaze with her eyes and cheeks, so that the cross blazed and glowed in that violent blizzard, without a single ray of sunlight.

"How I longed then, Marina, after that torture, Marina, do you remember that terrible exclamation: 'Father, hurry up, a second dead man is waiting at the gate!' It was as if he himself had come there and stood with his coffin on his shoulders, as if he had carried his own coffin, Marina!

"Marina, I really wanted to go home with you then—aching and howling—to soothe myself after all this death—no matter where home was. Somewhere I could be alone with you, and put my head on your lap—like I am now—and I would tell you everything about Yura, and give him to you right away, if you'd only take my head in your hands, and stroke me very gently, and tell me everyone hasn't died yet, that I did not die yet—like the rest. . . . Oh, how I envied Vakhtang Levanovich, walking with you arm in arm, putting his hand on your shoulder on the long road. He walked with you alone, in your brown fur coat, which at times—because of the wind—you seemed to envelope him, so much so that he seemed to be walking with you in the same fur coat and that you loved him!

"I then told him: 'Vakhtang Levanovich, why didn't you invite me to go with you? You are not a true friend.' He said: 'But, Sofia Evgenievna, I was walking with Marina Ivanovna.'

"'That's exactly what I mean, that you were walking with Marina Ivanovna!' (he, protesting:) 'But . . . I didn't know, Sofia Evgenievna. How could I know that you'd suddenly want to go with me!'

"'Not with you, you crazy man, with her: that it was *you* walking with her—and not me!!'—Marina, he was terribly offended, called me a big actress and some other thing . . . But I had to say it—with all my heart. On the other hand (blissfully serious eyes looking up at me)—two months later—maybe to the day—I was with you, not next to you on the street, but very close. I was looking at you intently with my eyes, and embracing you in my arms. It was warm out, not cold, and we were not going anywhere. We were just saying goodbye—I was already there with you. Now we've already arrived. I won't leave you, Marina, anywhere—never . . ."

Novodevichy Cemetery no longer exists. It is no longer in a suburb, now it's in the center of town. I have no doubt the original crystal cross still shines in another cemetery, but its neighbor is there, the simple oak cross?

Volodya, like me, loved everything old. He also astonished everyone around him with the "novelty" of his opinions, and also by putting this novelty in mock quotation marks—funny. He loved everything old, but in a youthful way. Old, but not decrepit. Both old world and new zealots misunderstood him. Old—in his own way—a past that never existed. This is also why he felt so good when he was with me, and even from our first meeting at the house of that cheeky, naughty lady with the arms and legs, I noticed he had on his finger a large antique silver ring—with a seal. Later I asked: "Where did you get this from? Is it yours . . ."

"No, Marina Ivanovna, it's not a family piece—I bought it by chance, because of my initials: V. A. (Pause). But if it was Zavadsky's he'd clean his up with chalk. And he wouldn't notice what was on it, because it was Chinese. Don't you think chalk is cheap? I don't clean mine with chalk, I like it when the silver blackens, when it's dark—mysterious like it's meant to be."

("And Zavadsky would clean his," meaning mine, and Volodya knew it. The chalk image immediately turned into a nine-line verse:

Sitting lazily in an armchair
I get up and kneel next to you—
Awaiting further orders,

Your hand hangs from sleepy armchairs
I take it without a sound
Hand adorned in a Chinese ring

Polished with chalk is the ring
Are you happy? What do I care!
My love has taken me over.[VIII]

The phrase "What do I care," I later changed in the handwritten book of poems I gave to him: "I had nothing to do with it . . .")

For Yuri Z. a Chinese ring; silver for Pavlik A.—the German one, cast in gold, taken from a prisoner or someone captured or killed in the war. The setting had roses in gold: with the gold hidden. There was this poem:

I give you a ring of iron:
Insomnia—rapture—despair.
So you do not look at girls' faces,
So you do not forget the word—tenderness.

So your head, covered in wild curls
Bubbling like a foamy goblet up to the sky,
Turns to embers—and ash—and-dust
Transforming this for you—this iron jewel.

When love itself approaches your
Prophetic wild curls—glowing ember,

Then be silent and press to your lips
The iron ring on your dark finger.

Here's the talisman from my red lips,
Here is the first link in your chain—
So that in the torment of days, you resist—
Alone like an oak tree—an iron encircled god.
(Moscow, March 1919)

***

I don't know what happened to the Chinese ring (I only know: I was the first to give him a ring!), the fate of the cast iron one is as follows:

Time passed and one day he came over—but there was no ring. "Is it lost?"

"No, I gave it to be cut, that is, to be split into *two*. (Pavlik's smaller!) Two wedding rings. Because I'm marrying Natasha."

"Well, I hate you! And the poems too, cut in two?"

After that, we saw each other less. There was no ring. "Where is the ring, Pavlik, or, the half-ring?"

"Marina Ivanovna, it's bad! When they cut it, both turned out too thin, Natasha's gold one broke immediately. When I went down to the basement to get some coal, mine dropped and rolled away, and because it was just as black as . . . Well, it ended up in the stove, with the family soup. It's still a luxury to cook millet with the cast-iron rose ring from a prisoner of war!"

Volodya's fate—his very own—will be discussed later.

In addition to the ring, Volodya also had a pistol among the old things, "Spanish pistol," as we called it, and for love of him, I introduced this pistol into my "Adventure" and entrusted it to my (Casanova) Henrietta:

"Ah, and don't forget your gift,
the Spanish Pistol!"

He brought this "pistol" to me on New Year's Day and solemnly presented it to me because he, like me, could not bear to keep it if someone else passionately liked a thing he had.

I was forced to leave this pistol in Russia; bury it in the attic along with someone else's Maltese sword (which will be discussed later), or rather its body remained in Russia, while I transported its soul, thanks to "The Adventure" across the border of time and visibility.

For this New Year, I wrote poems for all three of them together:

My friends! Dearest trinity!
More akin than kin!
In the Soviet night—Jacobin—
Marat's Moscow! My friends

With you, I begin with intense Pavlik A,
A favorite of the cold cold Muses,
Remember this—that I am named
For a Polish noble lady.

Blame me for this, the familiar cold
And a web of other shackles!
Guilty, forgetful—Yuri Zavadsky!
Most memorable of them all!

Finally—a hero among all actors
Declining the word's existence
All names forgotten—Volodya A!
He even forgot his own name!

So practicing the ancient art of
Disguising myself, a black diamond,
I listen to you sweetly and sadly,
Like the ancient Sibyl and Georges Sand.

It was at that moment that Volodya A. brought me his "pistol," January 1, 1919.

On this the New Year Day of 1919, which I celebrated with them, I offered the Third Studio—to all of them—my antique silver Greek king's mask, from the excavations. A mask is always tragic, but the king's mask is tragedy incarnate. I remember this happened in the theater. I remember the students organized a procession of thanks like the torchlight process (Fackelzug) for Bettina.[IX]

***

Like the ancient Sibyl—and Georges Sand . . .

Yes, yes, I felt for all of them, barely younger than me or the same age. I felt they were my sons, for I had already been married for a long time, and I had two children and two books of poetry—and so many notebooks of poetry! And left so many countries! It wasn't my marriage, nor the children, nor my notebooks, nor even the countries that I started recalling then. I started remembering when I began to live, but remembering means growing old, and despite my dazzling youth, I was old, old as a big rock that no longer recalls when it all started.

Since they were children—and actors, that is, doubly children, possessed by a single desire the one that was given to me. It was so easy for me, but so unnecessary, me alone, to have—a name or fame.

Oh, how I want to be famous! To walk and hear behind your back the whispers: "Look, there's . . . !"

But these were noble ladies whispering, Pavlik! Is it really so flattering?! If I were you, I'd quickly turn around and look at them like they were dogs: "Yes, it's Antokolsky! So what!"

They were all flattered by me, except Volodya. I loved them all. That's the big difference.

I never had any instinctive (maternal) tenderness for Volodya. Despite his youth, there was no young boy in him—neither boyish weakness nor boyish charm.

He had no magic: there was nothing inside of him, no warmth, no zest, no secrets, no enigma—he had a mission: before him—himself.

Because of this he couldn't be cold, nor hungry, nor fearful, he was incapable of being sad. And if all this happened to him (and it probably did), then it was not my business to prevent him, even gently, from overcoming the cold, hunger, fear, sadness, and from growing up.

The cool tenderness of a sister, confident in her brother's strength, because it was *her own strength*, and she bestowed it on him along his path. On all his paths.

***

It was Holy Saturday. Late evening. Devastated by the indifference of friends, the emptiness of the house, the emptiness of my heart (Sonya had disappeared, Volodya was not coming over anymore), I said to Alya: "Alya! When people are so abandoned by others as we are, there's no point imploring godlike beggars. He has enough of them even without us! Let's not go anywhere, not to any church, there won't be any 'Christ is Risen.' We will just lie down—like dogs!"

"Yes, yes, of course, dear Marina!" Alya babbled excitedly and trustingly, "And people like us, well, God should come to us! Because we're shy beggars, right? We are the ones who do not want to spoil his party!"

Shy or not, like dogs or not, we immediately lay down together on the bed—the servant's old bed, because at that time we still lived in the kitchen.

Now I'd like to explain the house a little bit. The house had two stories, and the apartment was on the second floor, but altogether there were three floors. I can't explain how and why, but it was like this: the lower floor with a dark hallway, two dark corridors, a dark dining room, my room, and Alya's huge nursery. The attic, actually two attics, one higher than the first one, there may have been four floors in all.

It was all so huge, spacious, neglected, deserted—and multiplied by the spaciousness and emptiness of it all. The attic created the general atmosphere, and it rolled down to the second attic, and then spread out to the entire place right down to its most remote and seemingly accessible corners.

In the winter of 1919, as I already said, Alya, Irina and I lived in the spacious, wooden kitchen, flooded by the sun, the moonlight, and—when the pipes would burst—by water. It had a huge stove, which we heated with scrap paper, belonging to some past tenant (ours had floated away, some adhesive paper was left, also—five thousand sheets of unsuccessful portraits of Rosa Luxemburg, and others—of French jackets and bloomers . . . all this remained—gathering dust, metamorphosing, until in flames).

So, it was eleven o'clock, the evening of Holy Saturday. Alya lay sleeping in her dress. I was also in a dress, but not sleeping. I was lying down burning up with bitterness—it was the first Easter in my life without "Christ is Risen," proof of my utterloneliness. I, who had made such effort all winter: the children, the queues, the trips to buy flour, where I almost lost my head at work in the People's Commissariat of Nationalities, the chopping, and the heating, and three plays written—I was starting the fourth—and so many poems—and such good ones—and I was a dog like no other . . .

Suddenly there was a knock. Light, sharp, quick. A commanding knock. I got up in one move, like a block—not collecting my arms and legs—but vertically. I bound through the dark kitchen, stairs, hallway, felt for the latch—and Volodya was on the threshold. I recognized his silhouette even in the darkness, he stood in the darkness.

"Volodya, is that you?"

"Yes, it's me, Marina Ivanovna, I came to pick you up—to go to matins."

"Volodya, come in now, I'll just get Alya up."

Upstairs, in a whisper (because it's a big mystery and because Christ has *not* yet risen): "Alya! Get up! Volodya has arrived. We're going to matins."

I smoothed her hair and mine in the darkness, and then took her down the dark night stairs . . . "Volodya, are you still here?"

Voice from the dining room: "I think so, it's so dark here, Marina Ivanovna, I don't even know where I am anymore."

We went out.

Alya, continuing to say what she started and left unfinished: "I told you, Marina, that God himself would come to us. But since God is a spirit and has no feet, we would die of fright if we saw him . . ."

"What? What is she saying?" said Volodya. We were already on the street.

Me, embarrassed: "Nothing, she's still sleepy . . ."

"No, Marina," a weak, distinct voice from downstairs, "I'm not sleeping, at all: since God himself could not come for us—to go to church, he sent Volodya for us so we would believe in him even more. Right, Volodya?"

"Of course, Alechka."

***

The Church of Boris and Gleb was ours. Round and white, like the eucharist bread. In front of this church, during service hours, soldiers were made to stand in line. Inside they celebrated, and outside they marched, but also celebrated. At this hour the soldiers were sleeping.

We entered a warm, diffuse light, a warmth of glowing candles and people. Women's voices sang, many voices were singing softly, and with great desire yet with such pain, it was hard to hear—so subtle, breaking, like a hair—just like the professor who said: "I have only one hair on my head, but it's thick . . ." Forgive me, Lord! Forgive me, Lord! Forgive me, Lord! I know this old priest: he recently celebrated mass with the patriarch, who came to the feast day in a black carriage—resplendent and fragile. Alya was the first to run up to him, simply to kiss his hand, and he blessed her . . .

"Marina Ivanovna, shall we go?"

We left with the crowd—only the old women remained.

"Christ is Risen, Marina Ivanovna!"

"He is *truly* risen, Volodya!"

***

Alya went home in Volodya's arms. Unaccustomed to children, he carried her awkwardly—not riding on his back, and not sitting on his arm, but rather, on his two outstretched arms, so that she was looking up at the sky.

"Alechka, are you comfortable?"

"I'm bless-ssed! This is the first time in my life I'm like this—lying down, like the Queen of Sheba on a stretcher!"

(Volodya did not expect this and stayed silent.)

"Marina, come here, I want to tell you something! I don't want Volodya to hear, because it's a great sin. No, no, don't worry, it's not what you think! It's really ok, but to God—it isn't!"

I go up to her. In a loud whisper she says: "Marina! Is it true that those nuns sang like a fly being sucked on by a spider? Forgive me, Lord! Forgive me, Lord! Forgive me, Lord!"

"What did she say?"

Alya, sitting up: "Marina! Don't repeat it! Because then Volodya will be tempted! This idea came from the devil—oh, Lord, what did I say again! I said an awful word!"

"Alechka, calm down!" said Volodya. (And to me: "Is she always like this?" Me: "Since birth.")

"We're already home, you'll be sleeping now, and in the morning when you wake up . . ."

Her hand holds a dark but obvious outline of an egg.

***

Alya came home and went to bed. I stood with Volodya at the door.

"Marina Ivanovna, is Alya fast asleep?"

"Completely. Don't be afraid, Volodya, she won't wake up!"

We went out along the Boulevard to the Moscow River. We stood on the quay (all of it like a dream)—we looked at the river . . . And now, as I write, I can still feel my ribs against the stone of the balustrade, on which we were both, for some unknown reason, strangely leaning, no doubt to make out something from the past? or the future? or an essence created within?

It was an evening of balustrades, railings, and bridges. We were constantly trying to see something and—and not having seen it here—we'd move to the next embankment, or the next bridge, as if there would be a specific spot—where everything would suddenly become clear in all four corners of the earth . . . Or maybe—it was saying goodbye to all of this: the Moscow River, the bridges, the places, the crosses? It seemed to me (and maybe I'm dreaming) that as we approached one of our observation points, and we encountered Pavlik walking away—he also was looking for the same thing. (On that Easter night of 1919, when all of Moscow was out in the streets and all, pretty much in the same place—around the Kremlin.)

Could they have been saying their goodbyes too? Our words that night, that long, long night, long ago, the many hours and many places—we were out at 1 a.m. and returned home in the full light of the late spring dawn. I don't recall our words on this night. This entire night was like one big gesture: from him towards me. An action not in words.

That night, looking out over the city, above one of those balustrades, with his shoulder next to mine, he made a decision that solidified within him, firmer than a rock, costing him more than his life. For me, it felt like an eternity—it was one hour of our friendship, like Aksakov would say, I would have given the rest of my declining days . . .

***

How did it all start? (For now, besides the bridges, it was a beginning.)

No doubt it was an accident, a happy coincidence, written in the stars, during one of her visits—at my house.

"What's this, Volodya, are you here? You also want to see Marina? I am jealous, Marina. So you're not here all alone when I am not here?"

"And you, Sonechka, do you stay alone when you are not here?"

"Me! I'm a lost cause, I am with everyone. I am so afraid of death that when there is no one there and no one can come over—those are terrible moments!—I am ready to climb out the window and onto the roof—just so I won't be alone: only not to die alone, Marina! And what are you doing here, Volodya?"

"Same as you, Sofia Evgenievna."

"So you love Marina too. Because I do nothing else—really, in the whole world. That's all I'm here for. And besides, I do nothing. And I don't intend to do anything else or be disturbed by other people either!"

"Sofia Evgenievna, I can leave. Do you want me to go, Marina Ivanovna?"

"No, Volodechka."

"And me. Should I go?" (challenged Sonechka).

"No, Sonechka. (A pause) And me. Should I leave?"

Laughter.

"Well, Marina, let's pretend he is not here. Marina! I came to see you on behalf of Yuri: believe it or not, he is getting another cold."

"I guess it means I have to write some poetry for him again. Sonechka, do you know the first poetry I ever wrote for him:

Handsome darkness, you are sad, you are sick:
The world is not just—a toothache! Tender
Shell-like cheek—silky scarf, nightlike . . .

Silky scarf? Scottish? Blue and black. I gave it to him—back then—a year ago! I remember very well, I had a neck scarf—I really love neck scarves, and this one especially! I came to him, and he had an abscess—I love it when people are sick! And especially when they are handsome—then they are kinder . . . (pause) . . . when a leopard is dying, he becomes kind: good-natured boy!! and he has such a terrible ugly headband—a knitted one—from a nanny, and me, not taking any time to think about it . . . Later I felt remorseful: it was my father's scarf, I have so little left of my father . . .

"Sonechka, do you want me to take it back? I could steal it?"

"What are you talking about, Marina, he loves it terribly now: he wears it when he has an abscess!"

Volodya, thoughtfully: "It is not a civilized man's disease, Sofia Evgenievna."

"What do you mean? Fool!"

Volodya, again: "Because it comes from a neglected tooth, and neglected teeth, in our time . . ."

"Go to hell: with dentists! Uncivilized disease! Are there any civilized diseases? Illness is fate: a person must die from something, otherwise he would live forever. Illness is destiny—always, but your civilization began yesterday and ends tomorrow, it's already over, because look how we are all living? Marina tears down her mahogany cabinets with her own hands for a fire so she can cook a bowl of millet. Is this civilized?"

"But Marina Ivanovna remains civilized even while breaking down cabinets."

"Which I never was. Is it true, Marina, that you've never been a civilized being?"

"Never, Sonechka. Even in a dream."

"I knew it, because all of it: the poems, Marina herself, the blue lantern, and this stuffed animal fox are magical and uncivilized. A civilized man—Marina!—this is almost as stupid as calling her a poetess. That's awful! Oh, how stupid you are, Volodya, how stupid!!"

"Sofia Evgenievna, you just told me that I was a fool, and stupidity is worse than that, so you're diluting your impression."

"And you are still deepening my anger. Because I'm terribly angry with you, with your presence, which you and Marina don't get, you're an actor, you should be in your studio . . ."

(Pause.)

"I don't know who you are to Marina, but—but I know Marina loves me more. Right, Marina?"

(I take her hand and kiss it.)

"Well, that's like I said it—more. Marina would never kiss your hand. And if you tell me she did kiss it . . ."

(Volodya: "Sofia Evgenievna!!")

"It's only out of pity, because you're a man, an ignorant creature, an inanimate object, the only inanimate being in all of Russian grammar. I know how we kiss your hand! Marina talked about this once. So once and for all: my ta-ta-ta-ta . . . Forgive my tears—my mediocrity and your divinity! But look—Marina, really?—isn't divinity *first*, and then—mediocrity! (Almost cries.) And Marina, if I should ask you, you'll get rid of him. Right, Marina?"

Me, kissing the other hand: "No, Sonechka, I won't."

"And if you don't, you're being polite, well-mannered, well-bred. She was educated abroad but in her heart she's already kicked you out. The moment I came in, she kicked you out. And please get out of this place, this is my place."

"Sonechka, you are such a devil today!"

"And you think I'm always silky, velvety, chocolaty, sweet, with everyone—like I am with you? Wow! Didn't Vakhtang Levanovich tell you I was a devil? I am. In any case, I'm mad. Volodya, do you know how to start up the gramophone?"

"I can, Sofia Evgenievna."

"Please start it up, whatever is on there is ok, I don't want to hear myself talk anymore."

What came on was *Ave Maria*—by Gounod. Then I saw a miracle with my own eyes: how music rose above the demon. The wild cat with extended claws and bared teeth, which Sonechka was from the moment she saw Volodya, disappeared with the first musical notes and dissolved into her immense eyes, no longer distinguishing me and Volodya. Her tears welled up in response—and then gushed:

"My God, what is this, I know it must be some kind of paradise."

"It's the *Ave Maria*, Sonechka!"

"Can this really be on the gramophone? I thought it only had 'Dance of the Apaches' on it or a tango."

"This is my gramophone, Sonechka, it has everything. Volodya, turn the record over."

The back of the record had a solo violin by Glinka, no lyrics, with the clearly spoken verses—by the great Baratynsky.

"Marina! I know that one too! Papa played it when he was still healthy . . . I fell asleep to it throughout my early childhood! "Do No Tempt Me for No Reason" . . . and how wonderful it is that it's—for no reason. You don't say that in life, you only say it *there*, where no longer any reason for anything exists—in paradise, Marina! And now I myself am in paradise, Marina, we are all in paradise! The fox is in paradise, and the wolfskin rug is in paradise, and the lantern, and the gramophone . . ."

"But, Sofia Evgenievna, in paradise," said Volodya's quiet voice, "there is no jealousy, and everyone has forgiven one another, because they saw there was nothing to forgive—there was no fault. And no reserved seats: everything is in its place. And now, Marina Ivanovna, I will leave."

Sonechka is in tears: "No, no Volodya, come on, you can't leave—after this music, it would be lonely—after such music, leave Marina—after such music . . . (a pause, barely audible:)—leave me . . .

"I could never forgive my behavior today. I thought you were nothing but empty beauty—and you too went straight to Marina's place, so she could write you some poetry and then you can boast about it!"

"Marina Ivanovna did not write me one poem! Right, Marina Ivanovna?"

"Yes, that's right, Volodechka."

"So, Marina, does that mean you are *not* in love with him?"

Half-kidding, I said: "I love him so much that I can't even put it into words. Or say it in poetry—I just can't."

"Less or more than Yura?"

(Volodya: "Sofia Evgenievna!" She: "Forget you're in the room: I really need to know this—now.")

I: "Volodya is my lifelong friend, but Yuri Alexandrovich was not my friend even for an hour. From the moment I met Volodya I called him simply, Volodya, but Yuri Alexandrovich—never Yura by itself, except in quotation marks or in absentia."

Concentrating but with a pained look, Sonechka says: "So—more or less? More or less?"

"Volodya—no comparison. Period."

"Now, Marina Ivanovna, I will really go."

***

And so it began. Just as before, they never met at my place, now they began to meet there constantly, perhaps because Volodya came less often before. Now he began to come every other evening, and towards the end—every evening—for things were clearly heading towards an end, still named but already known.

The departures began with Irina.

"Dear lady, let me take Irina with me to the village—look how puny she is. Come on, can't we give her Soviet milk? (That's what the children in Moscow called water in 1919.) But here in the countryside we have white milk, like under the Tsar, and real potatoes, not frozen, and bread without plaster. And Irina will come back to you—wait till you see!

The kitchen. The sun shining into both windows. Nadya the nanny from Vladimir, thin as a pole, with Irina dressed up in her arms. In front them is Sonechka, who has come running to say goodbye.

"Well, Irina, go and grow up big, beautiful and happy!"

"Irina with a mischievous smile: "Gally-da! Gally-da!"

"May your little cheeks get pink, may these little eyes never cry, may the hands that pick you up never let go, may your little legs run free and never fall . . ."

Irina, who has never seen tears, at least not like these, catches them unceremoniously rolling out of Sonechka's eyes.

"Wet, wet eyes, eyes, wet, wet . . ."

"Yes, they're wet, because they are tears . . . These are tears. But don't say it, please, better you don't know about them."

"Miss Sofia Evgenievna, we have to get on the train, Irina and I will not get there on time. We are on foot."

"Of course, Nanny, of course. What else could I tell her to make her understand? Yes, Nanny, let her certainly pray to God, every morning and every evening, just like this: Save us, oh Lord, and have mercy on dad, mom, Alya, Nanny . . ."

Irina: "Gally-da! Gally-da!"

"Gally-da, because she never called me Sonya, and I don't want her to forget me, I've never loved a child as much as I loved you in my life. (God will see to it!)—Nanny, don't you forget."

"Of course not, Sofia Evgenievna, Irina herself will remember, she'll be all abuzz with her Gally-da . . ."

Irina was understanding some of this and said with such amazing excitement: "Gally-da, Gally-da, Gally-da, Gally-da, Gally-da . . . (and with some mischievousness too:) Dalliga, Dalliga, Dalliga . . ."

"God be with you, Irina! You'll invoke Baba Yaga[X]! And you say—she'll forget! Now she won't calm down all the way there. Well, say goodbye, Sofia Evgenievna, otherwise we'll really be late!"

"Well, goodbye, my girl! Little hand . . . the other hand . . . little leg . . . the other leg . . . little eye . . . the other eye . . . little forehead—and that's all, don't kiss on the lips, and you, Nanny, please tell her the teacher has forbidden it—period—that's all.

"Well, goodbye, my girl! (Blesses her three times.) I will pray for you too. Get better, come back healthy, beautiful, rosy! Nanny, take care of her!"

***

I must say right now that Irina never saw her Gally-da again, and Gally-da never saw her Irina again. This was their last time, June 7, 1919.

Five months later, after leaving Sonechka, Irina, when she was two years and three months old, still remembered her as Gally-da, as we see from Alya's journal—of November 1919:

We have one friend who is not in Moscow. Her name is Sofia Evgenievna Gollidey. We call her Sonechka right to her face, and Sonechka Gollidey behind her back. Irina fell in love with her. Sonechka left her before, but Irina always remembered her, and still sings: Gally-da!

***

"Volodechka, haven't you ever been to Marina's kitchen?"

"No, Sofia Evgenievna, except once for Easter."

"Lord, you're so deprived! And you never met Irina?"

"Never, Sofia Evgenievna, only once—but she was asleep."

"Lord, how can you be friends with a woman and not know how many teeth her child has? You probably don't know how many teeth Irina has."

"I don't, Sofia Evgenievna."

"So, is this purely intellectual, you just want to be friends with Marina's head. Lord, who has only one part to them?!"

"You and I, Sofia Evgenievna."

"What a fool! I said: one part, a head—and nothing in it . . . Oh, that's in Ruslan and Lyudmila![XI] That kind of relationship would feel so cold to me! A house of ice . . . How much happier I am, Volodya! I also have the downstairs of Marina, the crystal part, and the lantern, under a blue light as if under water, because this is the bottom of the sea, and all the guests are monsters! and the upper Marina is over the stove, cooking millet, that ax, with the crooked brown hem of her torn dress, which—here—I'll kiss it!—my dear one, I adore her! And these two are Marina, they are all Marina, and, Marina, I don't see you now—only in the castle, at the top of the tower . . ."

"In the time I have left after the tower, I would probably tend the sheep . . ."

Volodya: "And you'll be hearing voices."

***

From the way things developed between Sonechka and Volodya, I began to understand from afar why men didn't love her. Every misunderstanding, every contradiction, every modest personal opinion, however harmless, invariably evoked these words: what a fool! And it was as if the word fool had already been fully charged and was just ready to go when the signal was given, anything could set it off. With her you needed to be patient—it required Volodya's impenetrably patient attitude.

***

I always walked her back to the right, towards Povarskaya Street, the departing Sonechka was leaving—the glowing Povarskaya Street at breaking dawn, a white street with no shops, resembling a river—as if there was nothing to the *left* of my house.

Only once it was different: at night, when it suddenly dawned on me that I had not yet given Sonechka my fountain.

The playful moonlit square was completely empty—in the daytime it was unkempt, Dog Square, but now it was like Seville Square, where the only moving thing was a round dance of trees, a slender silver stream, doubly silver: to the ear and to the eye, all at once . . .

"Is that a fountain, Marina?"

"It's *Marina's* fountain, Sonechka! Because in this house Pushkin read *Boris Godunov* to Nashchokin."

"I don't like Godunov. I love Don Juan. Everything is so round here, all around, quite round!"

It was as if the wind had carried everything away, and brought it back with a wave—without the participation of one's legs—we were already in the middle of the square.

And so, raising her hand to the shoulder of an invisible and very tall dancer, trustingly placing her left hand in his hand, slightly throwing her waist back on *his* invisible left one, slightly rising up on her toes because there weren't any heels then, twirling in a white dress and then twirling me around with it . . .

She danced like this around the fountain, but this was not a fountain, it was a memorial urn, it was an urn dance, the dance of death . . .

Das Mädchen und der Tod. [Death and the Maiden][XII]

***

"Marina, everything I have is diminutive, everything is diminutive, all my girlfriends, things, cats, even the men—all sorts of Katenkas, kitties, little nannies, Yurochkas, Pavliks, now—Volodechka . . . It's like I can't call anything big, I just can't. I only have you—*Marina*, so enormous . . . Oh, Marina! You are my magnifying glass."

***

Sonechka often thought ahead, I could see this in her absent, utterly sleepy eyes, eyes—noticing something for the first time ("Does this really happen—these blizzards, this love . . .").

Then she would totally freeze and her voice would become monotonous, unintelligible, and sleepy too, like her eyes; a voice that mothers lull their children to sleep with, and children lull themselves. (Mothers too.) And if she responded on cue—to me or Volodin—she seemed absent, as if in a dream, without intonation in her voice, like a sleepwalker. No, it wasn't really that she was thinking out loud but rather dreaming out loud.

"There's one person I never loved—he was a monk. Didn't have the chance."

"Ugh, Sonechka!"

"No, Marina, don't worry—I'm not talking about a bearded Orthodox one, but a clean-shaven one: a Catholic one, that is. Maybe quite young, maybe old—it doesn't matter. In a huge monastery, cold as a cellar. This monk lived alone—there was a plague, and everyone else died, decimated, he alone remained—to do God's work . . . One out of the entire order. The last one. The order is him alone."

"Sofia Evgenievna," Volodya's sober voice said, "let me tell you that a monastery does not represent the entire order. An order cannot disappear when all the monks in one monastery die. A monastery may disappear, but not an order."

"It was the last of the entire order, because all the monasteries have died out . . . Two thousand three hundred and thirty-three monasteries have died out, because of the Middle Ages and the plague . . . And I, I am a peasant woman in a white scarf and a striped skirt, and in such a nice corsage—with crossed ribbons—and I am the only one who survived in the whole village—because the monks caught the plague and contaminated everything (oh, Marina, I'm madly afraid of it! I mean the Catholic ones: they are strange birds, devils!)—and I bring milk to the monastery: milk from the last goat that has not yet died, I simply place it at the threshold of his cell."

"Does your monk drink milk?" Volodya with curiosity. "Because there are periods of fasting . . ."

". . . And then one day I come over—and yesterday's milk has not been touched. With a beating heart, I enter the cell—the monk is lying there—and that's when I see him for the first time: very young—or already a little old, but shaved—and I love him madly—and then I get it—it is the plague.

(Suddenly jumping up, she loses the thread and is wide awake.)

"No! I mean, the whole story was already over. He didn't have time to love me, because when there's a plague, there's no time for love. No, it's not like that at all. First there's love, then the plague! Marina, how can we make it come out right—*like that*?"

"You have to see the monk on the eve of the plague. On his last normal day. One day is a lot, Sonechka!"

"But how would I know that he would get the plague the next day? And if I didn't know, I wouldn't dare tell him, because I'd be telling him only because he's about to die, and he'd listen to me only out of mortal weakness!"

Volodya, contemplatively: "The plague begins with a runny nose. And sneezing."

"This is the doctor's plague: they sneeze, but mine is Pushkin's plague, no one sneezes there. But everyone drank and kissed each other. So how about it, Marina?"

"Go to him for confession: you must confess everything, and he must listen. It's not a sin, just a Christian duty."

"Oh, Marina! What a genius you are! So, I come to his chapel—he stands there in prayer—the only one of his entire order—and I kneel down . . .

(Volodya says: "He's on his knees, and you're on your knees? It's not right. Your foreheads will bump together.")

"He gets up and I do too, from my knees and I say: 'My Brother, I am a great sinner!' And he asks: 'But why?' And I say: 'Because I love you.' And he: 'God commanded us to love everyone.' And I: 'No, no, not like everyone else, but more than everyone, and no one else, and even more than God!' And he: 'Oh-oh-oh! Dear sister, I can't hear anything you said, there's a huge wind in my ears, and I'm starting to get sick with the plague!' Suddenly he staggers—and collapses—I support him, and I feel his heart beating through his frock, beating madly! beating madly! to the point of breaking!—and so I lead him, I lead him out of the chapel, not into a cell, but onto the green meadow, and there's a tree, the first one blooming—and I sit down with him under the blooming tree—and I put his head on my lap . . . and quietly I hum to him . . . the *Ave Maria*, Marina! I get weaker and weaker, because I also have gotten the plague, but God is merciful, and we do not suffer, and I have a beautiful voice—Lord, what a voice I have! and not just one tree is blooming, but all of them, because they are in a hurry, they know that we have the plague!—a whole procession of flowers, as if we were getting married!—and we are no longer sitting, but walking, hand in hand and not on the ground, but a little above the ground, above the daisies, and the further we go, the higher we are, we are already half a meter from the ground, a meter already, Marina! Then two meters! and now we are already walking above the trees . . . And above the clouds . . . (Very quietly and inquisitively:)—Is it possible to go—above the stars?"

Rubbing her eyes with all her heart: "So, Marina, I did love a monk!"[XIII]

***

". . . And I have to live with people, who are so different! The monk immediately understood everything—and forgave everything—and warded everything off without me saying anything. But, Marina, as much as I go on explaining, bending over backwards, to the point of losing my sight, my voice, my skin—no one understands, not even Evgeny Bagrationych—with his notorious talent for 'fantasy!'

"However, he has some good reasons for this. At the very beginning there was a terrible scandal with him. We started talking about images and characters in the Studio."

"Images, Sonechka!"

"Well, about images, you know. To be the image. Some can be images, some not, and so on. And I said: 'And Evgeny Bagrationych, in my opinion, conforms to the image of Pechorin.' Everyone said: 'That's nonsense! Pechorin[XIV] was from a hundred years ago, and Evgeny Bagrationych is modernity itself, the theater of the future, and so on.' I reply: 'So, I didn't understand, I wasn't talking about ideas, but his face—man was created in the image and likeness. Because, in my opinion, Evgeny Bagrationych is terribly similar to Pechorin: the same nose, the same chin, and the same hemorrhoidal face.'"

I said: "What?"

Sonechka, meekly: "That's it, Marina, word for word, in those words. Suddenly there were howls, everyone pounced on me, even Evgeny Bagrationych: 'Sofia Evgenievna, there are limits to everything—even your expressions.' And I insisted: 'What is offensive here? I've always read it in Chekhov and Potapenko, and there's no problem with them at all—since they're such great writers . . .' 'And what do you think hemorrhoidal means?' 'Oh, yellow, bilious, bitter, dejected—hemorrhoidal.' 'No, Sofia Evgenievna, it's not yellow, bilious, bitter, and not proud, either, it's a disease.' 'Yes, yes, terrible, a liver disease, that's probably why I said Pechorin.' 'No, Sofia Evgenievna, this is not a liver disease, but hemorrhoids—haven't you ever read about it in the newspapers?' 'Of course, I read about it.' 'No, please, leave it out of course, because in the newspapers there are so many diseases and one is more unpronounceable than the other. *My* advice to you is before you speak . . .' 'But I really had a sense of this word! It seemed so melancholy to me, so magical, so completely yellow, almost brown—like you!'

"Then later someone explained it to me. Oh, Marina, it was so horrible! And most importantly, I used the word so often in my life and then I couldn't remember about whom . . .

"It seems to me Evgeny Bagrationych in the end couldn't believe I didn't know. That is, he knew, but, in a way, he lost confidence in me. When I *really* wanted to say something—and with me it was always obvious!—he'd watch my mouth—looking so disapproving and high and mighty—well, just like a snake staring at a bird! As if—with a glance—he could immediately close my mouth! If he could, he'd clamp it with his hand!"

***

More about words.

"Everyone here says: Revolution . . . Revolution . . . But I don't know . . . It's just that some words and terms are so strange: a card for consumption sounds like a long-distance ship, I immediately see wa-a-a-ter, and nothing else but water. Yes, nothing but water. And—for example: closed distribution center?

This sounds like a deaf old man, tightly closed, I'd say to him: 'Grandfather!' and he'd say: 'Huh?' 'Dis-distribution, please!' and he: 'Heh-heh!' and so on for hours . . . And also *zhagra*: sounds like plague, epidemic, scurvy, but it's just tea made from dried carrots."

***

". . . Marina! Why do I love bad poetry so much—while I also love yours so much, and that of Pavlik, and Pushkin, and Lermontov . . . The midday heat, Marina, how it *scorches*! I always feel like I am both a he and a she, and I'm lying down, Marina, in the valley of Dagestan, with smoke rising from my wound, and at the same time, Marina, I'm in a circle of friends, alone yet pensive . . ."[xv]

And in a wonderful dream my young heart
God knows why—I'm *endlessly* drowning . . .

"All the poems in the world are written about me, Marina, for me, Marina, to me, Marina! That's why I never regret not writing them myself. Marina, you are a poet, tell me, does it really matter who it's about? Is there anyone really? (Listen, listen, listen, I'm getting confused! But you understand!) Marina, did you really write all this? I know your hand, I look at it and I can hardly restrain myself from kissing it—in public, not because these idiots would see it as a sign of servility, schoolgirl sentimentality, or hysteria, but because you, Marina, need to be kissed—in front of everyone, past, present and future, and not only in front of three or four acquaintances. If that other night, not meaning to, during that Dickensian night, I kissed you in front of Pavlik, it was out of weakness, Marina, I simply could not restrain myself—restrain my gratitude. But Pavlik doesn't count, Marina—he is a poet—a bit like a little dog, I want to say that he is not quite a person—(and you, Volodya, don't count either: you watch—and—I kiss her in front of you, but you don't count—because I've already decided: when the three of us are together, Marina, we are alone . . .) And what about in front of everyone, at the S.'s—it's worse, but you wonderfully pushed away that fox terrier—given his own back without flinching . . . Marina, I kiss your hand—for your hands—for your entire self—not just for the poems alone, but for the wardrobes and shelves you took down—even more! I am always upset when they say that you are a remarkable poet, and most of all when they say that you are 'brilliant.' Pavlik is brilliant, because he has nothing else, but you have everything, you are everything. Don't get hurt, Marina, but you are not just your poems, compared to what you are—they are just a little nibble of what you are, such a pitiful little crumb! I just find it funny when they call you a poet because you are so much more. Although there is no more superior word than poet, your vocation—your calling in life is greater. These other things are you, too. All these things are you. If you never wrote poetry, not a single line, if you were deaf and dumb like me and the *Little Mermaid*—you would still be you, the same person: only with your mouth sewn shut. And—I would love you—not more, because more doesn't exist, but in exactly the same way—on my knees."

(My face was buried in my knees:)

"Marina! Do you know what my greatest accomplishment is? Even more than my time with that red-nosed one (the organ grinder), because it was more difficult not to be with him than to be with him, after *Blizzard*—but not having kissed your hand! Not servitude, no, not for fear of people's eyes—but for fear of losing you, Marina, fear of suddenly losing you, or of suddenly conquering you (what a horrible word! conquer, grab, acquire, obtain—all of them horrible!), or the opposite—fear of you,

Marina, well, a terrible fear, like what we call fear of God,—but no, it's not that: fear—of turning the key, of swallowing poison—of something starting up that cannot be stopped . . . Fear of doing this, Marina! 'Open, Sesame!' Marina, then forgetting the word to go back! Never being able to get out of this mountain again . . . And be buried alive in the mountain . . . Which also could fall down upon you. . . .

"And simply—a fear of your fear, Marina. How am I supposed to know? All my life, Marina, I thought I was the only one like this: words, actions, and thoughts—the only one, and suddenly I had neither word, nor action, nor thought, only some kind of electric flash!

About *Blizzard*: when I heard this verse, in my own ears:

Prince, is this a dream or a sin?
Poor frightened bird!
I am first—before anyone!—
I heard your little bells!

"This very emphasis: *first—before anyone*, the same insistence, as if it was taken from my mouth—Marina! Inside me—everything trembled, I shook alive (you're going to laugh)—my whole stomach, my entire digestive tract, all those mysterious insides that no one ever sees—all that I had inside me—from my neck down to my knees—a mass of fine pearls, and suddenly all of it came to life.

"And there you have it, Marina, while loving your poems so much, I also madly, madly, hopelessly, horribly, shamefully, love—the bad ones too. The really bad ones! I'm not talking about Nadson (I bow before him!) and not Apukhtin (for his Dark Eyes [Ochi Chornye]!), but those, Marina, who no one composed but everyone knows by heart. Do you know, like the poems from *The Poetry Reader*, Marina?[XVI]

He picked her up from the mud,
He started stealing, to please her.
She bathed in contentment
She laughed at the madman.

From prison he beseeched her:
I'm heartbroken without you!
She flew off in a troika
She laughed at the fool.

And in the end, they took him to a hospital, and—
He was dying. She was dancing
She drank wine and had fun.

(Oh, I could kill her!) Even when he had died and was being taken to the cemetery, she—

She walked behind the coffin laughing!

"But perhaps I made this up myself in order to hate her even more, because I've never seen anything like it: someone following a hearse and laughing out loud, have you?

"But perhaps you think these are ones—the bad ones? Then listen carefully. Oh, Lord, I forgot! I forgot! I forgot! I forgot how it begins, I only remember the end!

And the count was devilishly handsome!
. . .
And I sharpened my knife in the dark,
And the count was devilishly good-looking!

Wait, wait, wait!
A red curtain flew up:
In his arms was his sister!

That's when she kills them both, and in the last verse, the sister lies down and we see her face with a horrible grin, and—the count was devilishly good-looking!

Do you know "The Pale Tea Rose"? He meets her in the park, or maybe in church, and she's sixteen and she's wearing a white dress . . .

And a pale tea rose
Shivered on your chest.

Then, of course, she throws herself into debauchery and he meets her in a restaurant, with some soldiers, and suddenly she sees him!

The tears in your eyes trembled,
You shouted: "Quick! Quick!"
And a pale tea rose
Shivering on your chest.

Days passed in succession,
I was looking for joy in oblivion,
And once again in front of me
Your earlier beloved gaze gleamed.

Prosaic family life suffocated you,
You walked surrounded by children,
And a pale tea rose
Shivered on your chest.

"And then she is dead, Marina, and lies in a coffin, he approaches the coffin and sees this:

Tears frozen, in your eyes . . .
—and I no longer know what rhymes with eyes or chest—

And a pale tea rose
Shivered on your chest.

"Shivering, you realize her chest was no longer breathing! And—I adore all of this madly: the crowd of children and the dubious joys and the pale tea rose and the grave.

"But that's not all, Marina. It's still somehow bearable, because it's so sad. And there are some really stupid things that I love madly. You know that?

I was born
Baptized
Married
Blessed.

She gave birth.
Baptized the baby
Was married off
Blessed, then
She died.

And that's all—a woman's life!
And you, you know this well.
My pen wrote
I don't know for whom . . .

I: My heart told me:
For my sweet friend.

Sonechka: Here is a little dog,
I pray you love her
She'll teach you
How to love a friend.

"Loving a friend—is this really poetry, Marina? I can write like this. I see a quill—certainly a goose quill, all chewed up, and the little dog, Marina, with curly ears, the color of silvery chocolate, and eyes that are about to cry: eyes that I myself have.

"Now, Marina, in conclusion, these are my favorites. I say this seriously. (Defiantly:) I lo-o-ove them more than yours.

The blue balloon is spinning, spinning,
Blue balloon, stay with me!
Spinning, spinning, it wants to fall,
A rider wants to carry off the young lady!

"No, Marina! I cannot! I have to sing it for you!"

(She jumps up, throws her head back and sings the same verse over again. Then comes up and stands over me:)

"Now tell me, Marina, do you understand me? Can you love a girl like me? Because these are my favorite poems. Because (closing her eyes) they are simply bliss. (Reciting, as if in a trance:) Balloon—in the blue sky—spinning, spinning, a hot-air balloon, a mesh of blue silk, itself is blue—the sky too is blue, and the other one looks at it and is insanely afraid that the balloon will fly away! And his glances make the balloon spin even faster and is about to fall, and the whole hot air balloon will perish! Now we take advantage of the fact that he is busy with the balloon . . .

Gentleman wants to steal a young lady!
What can be added to this?

And here's Sonechka:
The curtain trembled gently.
The room welcomed the footsteps
Of the Blue cavalier
And the servant . . .

"Everything is here for you, except the young lady—and the ball. But the ball, Sonechka, which is *earthly* and it is moving away from the young lady. She's already behind, done. He has already taken her—and then realized there was no need for it."

Sonechka, jealously: "Why?"

I: "Because he was a poet who did not need to take in order to possess something. Who didn't need to possess."

"And if it was me, would he have gone too?"

No, Sonechka.

***

"Oh, Marina! How I love pain! Even a simple headache! Because I don't know anything about dentistry, I don't know about toothaches, I've never had one. Sometimes I'm ready to cry because I've never had a toothache—they say it's such a magnificent pain: so nagging!"

"Sonechka, you've lost your mind! Ugh, she can bring bad luck, the little devil! Do you know who Malibran was?"

"No."

"A singer."

"Did she die?"

"About a hundred years ago and she was young. Well, Musset wrote this poem to her—'Verses to Malibran'—listen:

(Changing some words for Sonechka:)

Didn't you know, you indiscreet actress,
That the frantic screams from your heart,
Increased the heat of your emaciated cheeks?
Didn't you know that on your burning forehead,
Your hand was getting warmer every day
And loving suffering means tempting God?

. . . Strange coincidences. The summer of 1937, at the ocean shore, when I was writing *Sonechka* in full swing, I picked up *Sixty Years of Memories* from a local bookshop, and also from the library. I also got the 1867 volume of the journal *Lectures*—and the first thing I saw was Ernest Legouvè's *Sixty Years of Memories—La Malibran* (about which I knew nothing until then, except for Musset's poems).[XVII]

"Despite the fact that she herself was life incarnate and one of the main feature of her character was charm, the thought of death never left her. She always said she would die young. There were times she seemed to feel a certain chill, as if the shadow world touched her soul; she fell into terrible fits of melancholy and her heart would drown in a stream of tears. I have here before my eyes her handwritten notes: Come to me immediately! I'm choking on my sobs! All these funereal visions were at my bedside and death was at the head." (*Sixty Years of Memories,* translated from French.)

***

Doesn't it seem like a little note from Sonechka?

***

There were unplanned meetings every evening. They arrived randomly, from different theaters and different times and ways of life. And Sonechka always wanted to stay a little longer and be the last one to leave, but since that would mean not going home with Volodya, I insisted that they leave together every time.

"Come on, Sonechka, otherwise I will inevitably have to go with you, and I'll probably disappear into your house, and Alya will go hungry and time will go by quickly—etc.!"

I was reassured and relieved to let them go—at dawn.

I sometimes walked with them, at dawn, to the corner of Boris and Gleb Lane and Povarskaya Street.

"Love each other, you who have both loved me, and sometimes say my name to one another when you kiss."

***

"Marina! So it turns out Volodya is in love! When people realized I was into him—because I was always talking about him: to get me to say his name—they immediately told me the other day in the Electric Cafe all night long he did not take his eyes off the dancer who was dancing on the table—and he didn't even finish his drink.

"When I found out, I immediately told him: Shame on you, Volodya, to go to Marina's and then go watch a dancer! Yes, Marina makes magical beings come out on her sleeves! You're such a fool! And I immediately told him that I would definitely tell you—and he got very scared, Marina, he turned all dark and flew into a rage! And do you know what he told me: I always thought you were like that only with Marina Ivanovna, and that it was she who was like you. And now I know. He left. Now look at how he'll come to you—all sheepish!"

He came not sheepish but preoccupied and immediately said:

"Marina Ivanovna, you must understand me correctly regarding Sofia Evgenievna, just like you've understood me correctly about everything up to now."

"Volodya! Didn't I explain Zavadsky to you? There's this fairy tale—a Norwegian one, I think—whatever the old man does—he does well. And the old man keeps getting into mischief. He exchanges a bar of gold for a horse, a horse for a goat, and so on, and, in the end, a cat for a bobbin, and a bobbin for a needle. He loses the needle at the house right when he climbs over the fence—because he didn't go through the gate. So let's be like the old man for each other, that is: as long as *he* feels ok! and returns home *safe*!—Especially since I am capable of gazing at a dancer for three minutes—as long as she doesn't speak.

"Volodya! But how awful would it be if we put the fairy tale—in reverse, namely, a needle for a bobbin, the bobbin for a sheep, and finally, the horse for gold? Oh, what a lousy old man he would be!"

"A terrible old man, Marina Ivanovna! All of Moscow is now full of such "old men" at the moment. It's to escape from them that I . . ."

"No, Marina Ivanovna, I didn't gaze at her—she made me think. Now, the world as we know it has collapsed; nothing remains of the old, and this is forever: a table—and on it a dancing void. A dancing—in spite of everything—the void—in spite of everything—these lessons."

"They say people love girls like that . . ."

"If I ever marry, it will only be to a nurse, so that humanitarian blood flows in the veins of my children."

***

Marina, if you only knew how Volodya kisses—so intense! So hard (with a mischievous grin)—like I'm a wall! My face has been aflame all day today.

***

To my great joy, I will say that he never made an attempt to explain his relationship with Sonechka to me. He knew that

I knew that it was the last way he had of taking a step closer to me. It was a rapprochement, not a separation, that when he kissed her, he was kissing me too, that he was kissing us all—himself, her, me—all three of us and throughout the spring of 1919 he kissed—in her person, her little face—he kissed.

Any attempt *to use words* would be a humiliation and the end.

And Sonechka? She babbled and babbled, adding, multiplying, conjugating, bending down, sowing and reaping, scattering Volodya far and wide with words, she simply rejoiced in him, innocently—as on the first day of creation.

***

We positioned ourselves like this: Volodya on the left, me on the right, Sonechka in the middle, both of us with Sonechka in the middle, like adults with a child in the middle, we who loved with our love in the middle. Embracing, of course: we stretched our hands to each other over her shoulders, she was within us, in our distant embrace, dividing us and bringing us closer at the same time, giving each one her hand and to each of us oneself, all of her love. With her small body, she filled the immense distance between me and Volodya.

Sonechka sat with us as if we were a chair with a living back—a wicker chair made of our intertwined hands. Sonechka lay on us as if in a cradle, like Moses in a basket on the waters of the Nile.

And from the dark corner, the gramophone, stretched out its cherry wood sounding horn towards us, singing and playing for us—everything it could, everything we knew: about our youth, our love, our melancholy, our parting.

And when, later, before leaving Russia, I sold the player to the Tatar, I sold part of my soul—my entire youth.

***

. . . Happy spring, never seen in this world . . .

That's how Pavlik's poems resonated in the three of us, spoken by another long since killed and buried—already an eternity ago!—I heard them in a dark train car.

Happy spring—never seen in this world!
Which Mozart or Rossetti brought to us
Joyful—babble—anachronistic flower—
Aimless spring—in the name of—Romanticism.

***

How long did they go on—these our sleepless nights together? My feelings say it was an eternity, but at the same time I also felt it was one single, endless, ephemeral night and strangely, not dark, or moonlit—although, probably there was a moon and it was dark—but there was no blue light glowing from a lantern that *no longer* lit, because all the electricity was cut off in springtime. Some kind of silvery, sprinkled, dream-like dawn—a real daybreak, with our faces flickering in the pale light, or maybe that was just in our memories—in the words of Sonechka:

"Marina! I realized that these are the real White Nights! Because now I, too, love two people. But why do I feel so good? What about you, Marina?"

"Because it's not really two people but both together, Sonechka! And me too—I love both of you. And I feel 'so good,' too. What about you, Volodya?"

"I feel *good* (with a deep sigh), Marina Ivanovna!"

***

"Sonechka, why don't you ever wear a necklace?"

"Because I don't have one, Marina."

"Here I thought you didn't like . . ."

"Oh, Marina! I would give my soul for a necklace—a coral one."

"Do you want me to tell you a fairy tale about a coral necklace? Well, listen. Her name was Ondine, and his name was Hans, a knight. A torrential storm swept him to the hut where she was living with an old man and an old woman. The torrent was her uncle—Uncle Stream that deliberately overflowed so much as to push the knight into the hut, making the hut into an island from which he could not leave. The same torrent brought an old priest to them, who married them and she received a living soul. She immediately changed: from soulless and happy to unhappy but in love—and I am convinced that from then on he began to love her less, although this is not in the fairy tale. He took her away to his castle—and began to love her less and less—and he fell in love with the Duke's daughter—Bertholde. So the three of them went to Vienna, on the Danube, and on the boat Bertolde was playing in the water with her pearl necklace—suddenly a hand came out of the water and with a devilish laugh—it grabbed the necklace! And the water all around was covered with hideous faces and the boat almost capsized. Then the knight became terribly angry, and Ondine put her hand over his mouth, begging him not to scold her on the water, for on the water her family were water spirits—and became very powerful. The Knight calmed down and Ondine leaned toward the water saying something flattering for a long time. And suddenly something came out—there!"

"Oh, Marina! What was it?"

"The necklace, Sonechka, Ondine's necklace."

A coral necklace—a gift my brother had brought me as a gift the day before.

"Marina! Look what I've brought you!" said my brother.

From his hand to the table and over the edge, it looked like a double cascade of huge stone grapes, elongated, a cherry-red color, polished like the lips of a child, oblong—barrel-like.

"They were selling them and I got it for you—even though you are blonde, you can wear it anyway, you won't ever find another like it."

"But what kind of stones are they?"

"Coral."

"Are they, really?"

"Yes, they are. But one more thing happened—right away: it became clear this was not happening to me. The whole evening I held them in my hands; weighing them, sorting them, rubbing them, touching my cheeks with them, my lips, counting them with my lips, going over them like a rosary, the whole evening saying goodbye to them, wondering who could be the owner of this splendor under this sky, then I knew it was . . ."

"Oh, Marina! Are these corals? So enormous? So dark? Are they yours?"

"No."

"What a pity! Whose are they?"

"Yours, Sonechka. They're for you."

And . . . not asking another thing, without closing her lips half-opened in amazement, as if they were in the middle of a word, petrified! Forgetting everything in the world, even me—she took them with both hands, with such concentration, with such fervor—and she put them on at once.

That's how Cosette, once upon a time, took the doll from Jean Valjean's hands:[XVIII] she was speechless and full of emotion.

"Oh, Marina! But they reach my knees!"

"Wait, when until you get old, they'll reach down to the ground!"

"I'd rather not grow old, Marina, because how can an old woman wear something like this?"

"Marina! I never understood the word happiness. With a fine pen—drawing a circle the size of the entire sky—inside there is nothing. Now I am—happiness itself. Me—plus the corals—an equal sign—happiness. And everything is solved."

Squeezing the necklace into her fist—as if one could squeeze them in a handful—a handful that could barely hold four beads, dripping, tangled, a kind of madness of fullness: she drinks it? Feast on it?—kisses it.

And then these strange words, at such a moment: "Marina! I really believe this is the last time I'll feel alive."

***

What the coral necklace was for Sonechka—Sonechka was for me.

***

"And what about the other necklace—Ondine's?"

"She held it out to Bertholde—in exchange for the *other* necklace but the knight snatched it from Bertholde's hands and threw it into the water, cursing Ondine and her entire family . . . and Ondine could no longer stay on the boat . . . No, it's too sad of an ending, Sonechka, you'll cry. Just know that this necklace is the same Danube necklace, taken from the Danube and returned to the Danube, a necklace of vanquished jealousy and posthumous fidelity, Sonechka, and male recognition . . ."

***

Our farewell began with these corals. The corals themselves were already a farewell. Do not give your loved ones something too beautiful; for the hand that gives and the hand that receives will inevitably part, as they have already parted—in the actual gesture of giving, a gesture that separates, not joins: empty hands on one side—full hands on the other. In the gap formed by the very gesture of giving and receiving—a whole space will rush in to make a separation, inevitably.

From hand to hand—you transmit a separation, it spreads with such corals!

After all, we give away such beautiful corals in place of ourselves, it is because of the impossibility of giving—ourselves, in compensation for ourselves—through these corals we take from the other person. There is a betrayal in such gifts. Not for naught do people with wise hearts fear them: "What will you take from me—if you give me such a gift?" Such corals are like a ransom: one brings a pineapple to a dying person, so as not to go into the pit with him. One brings roses to a convict, so as not to go with him to Siberia.

"Marina! I'm leaving with the Studio."

"Yes? For how many days? For a play?"

"Far away, Marina, for the whole summer."

All summer, but when you love someone—it's a whole lifetime.

Thus such gifts were always given as farewells: for departures, for weddings, for birthdays (that is, the same farewell: whether the year with the loved one, or a year of love.) Laden with this significance, they themselves end up causing the separation—then they came along with us and gradually became a symbol, then its signal, and then the embodiment: of the farewell itself.

Maybe if I hadn't given Sonechka the corals . . .

***

Fifteen years later, walking along Rue du Bac in Paris, somewhere in a little niche, in an antique shop window—I saw them again. A blow to my heart: displayed on the velvet breastplate where they were placed. Suddenly I saw them—and suddenly appeared the slender stem of her neck and her same small dark pink, brown-eyed face, with lips the color of dark cherry-red wine, and those same rays of light as on the stones. It was a brief vision. I looked again—it was dark again—now a green velvet breastplate had a label: a four-digit number.

***

After the corals, the dresses flowed out, chiffon and satin. It happened like this. We were walking along a dark corridor towards the exit and suddenly a thought came to me: "Sonechka, stop, don't move!"

I was diving down into the blackness of a huge wardrobe and I went back in time seventy-seven years ago—not seventy-seven but seventy and seven years ago, seventy and seven. A fantasy—with real feelings as in a dream—that something had long ago obviously fallen down because of its weight, swishing—had puffed up, settled, spread out, and spilled over—soaking in the puddle of silk, I am covered up to my shoulders.

"Sonechka! Here, hold this!"

"Oh, what is it, Marina?"

"Wait, wait!"

Another plunge into the abyss, and again my hand reached into the puddle. But this time it wasn't tin I was touching but mercury, liquid-like running off and playing in my hands. But I couldn't take it in handfuls because it leaked and flew away in all directions from my predatory fingers. For if the first [dress]—collapsed under its weight, the next one—flew off because of the lightness: leaving the hanger like it was a tree branch.

And following the first one, a sagging, brownish faille dress from the great-grandmother Countess Ledokhovskaya—the unfinished dress by her daughter, my grandmother, Maria Lukinichnaya Bernatskaya. Unfinished by her daughter—my mother—Maria Alexandrovna Main—who didn't have it made until it was finally made by the great-granddaughter—the first Marina of our Polish family—by me, my hands, seven years ago, in girlhood, but in the *style* of my great-grandmother: the bodice like a cape and the skirt like the sea:

"Now, Sonechka, wait!"

And on Sonechka, sagging under the weight of four generations of women—blue on top of brown: blue with purple, azure dress, madness, Turkish-style, market-like, scarlet-flowered—the dress itself was a flower.

"Marina!"

Sonechka staggers and above all, she does not see or understand anything, neither the blue color of the second one nor the chestnut color of the first—for the wardrobe is a cavern, the corridor is a coffin (Oh, these dark places of my former homes, the present, future ones . . . Oh, these dark houses! Don't my poetic obscurities come from you?—*I believe in nights!)*

Like a statue on wheels, I push Sonechka who is submerged in her dresses, from the complete obscurity of the corridor into the semi-darkness of the dining room: the ceiling, not cleaned for two years—and the world has passed us by—from the dining room to the next black corridor—a black parade of trunks, the black sea of the piano—and right up to Alya's nursery—a light! finally!

I place her, staggering and stupefied by the dark places, silent as a coffin, in front of a floor to ceiling mirror:

"Try it on!"

She squints as if she's just woken up, her black eyelashes flicker quickly—will she burst out laughing or cry . . .

"These are the dresses. Try them on, Sonechka!"

And now—an alternate vision—of paleness and penury: a white neckline in poor lace; the trim of the skirt, a chemise insert—the complete disappearance under the bell of the skirt—and, in the greenish water of the dawn in the mirror, in the double green of the dawn and the mirror—a new vision: a girl, great-grandmother—a hundred years ago.

Standing, intently fastening the tight-fitting bustier with all its twelve small buttons, she straightens and adjusts the smallest folds of the belt, and with her hand, guides them down to the huge waves of the hem . . .

I catch her eye—is it happiness? No, it's not happiness, but a terrible, childlike grave seriousness—a girl in front of the mirror. A look of deep inquisitiveness, checking all the facts (and what is not given!), a look of Columbus, Archimedes, Nansen. A look that lasts—maybe an hour?

And finally: "Wo—o—nderful, Marina! It's just a little long."

(Too long, meaning like those gigantic manes on the big Voronezh horses—you can't even see their noses!)

She stands there, already happy, flaming hot, bowing to herself in the mirror, and, taking three steps back, slightly lifts the sides of her robe, stiff because of its weight—and makes a deep curtsey from my great-grandmotherly time.

"But this dress is for a ball, Marina! I'm already floating! I can't even move and it's already floating by itself! It's dancing a waltz, Marina! No—the minuet! And will you let me wear it?"

"And what do you think?"

"Of course! And I'll stand at the back of my chair, this chair—remember how poor we were, Marina!—And the dress—it's not rich either, but it has a nobility. It's the one *Nastenka*[XIX] wore to go see *The Barber of Seville*! It was her grandmother's! (I'll have to introduce her!) Will you give it to me just for today, Marina? Because I still need time to hem it."

"For today—and for tomorrow—and forever and ever."

"Wha-at? Is it for me? But this is heaven, Marina. It must be a dream. You won't believe it, Marina, but this is my first silk dress: I was once young, then daddy died, then the Revolution . . . There were blouses, but never dresses. (A pause.) Marina! When I die, will you dress me in this? Because it was my first such happiness . . . I always thought that I loved white, but now I see that it was from a lack of imagination and poverty. Because there was nothing else. This is my color, it *suits* me, as you'd say. It's as if they threw me into a cauldron—all of me: my eyes, my hair, my cheeks—and boiled me, and what turned out was this. What do you think, Marina, for instance, if I got married in the provinces this summer—I know I won't get married, but if I did—could I get married in blue? Because—I was told—now they even get married in military garb—brides, that is. Can you believe one could get married in riding pants? That is, she wanted to get married in them, but the priest refused, so she gave up—a church marriage.

"It's decided, Marina! I'm getting married in blue, but when I'm in my coffin—I'll be in a chocolate color!"

***

After the dresses came the yellow chest.

After I knew she was leaving, I never left her side—I went with Alya to her in the morning and stayed for her remaining time there. (And from somewhere, in the depths of my hearing came the word: *regne* [kingdom, French]. In Canada, where to this day instead of *vie* [life, French] they say *regne*, about the humblest poorest human life, the life of a woodcutter and a raftsman—*regne. Mon regne. Ton regne.* So, in French Canadian, this is what remained of the life of Sonechka, like the succession of others, would have been a *regne, la fin de son regne* [The end of her kingdom/life, French]. Let no one accuse me of hyperbole.

A *great* people, so called—life.)

"Well, Marina, I'm packing my bags today!"

I was sitting on the windowsill. The green chair was empty; Sonechka unpacks and repacks, like a cat with her kittens, from one place to another she carries rags, pieces of paper, boxes . . . She opens a yellow chest. I also come over to finally look at her dowry.

The yellow chest was empty. At the bottom of the yellow chest there were only some new dazzling reddish children's shoes.

"Sonechka? Where is the dowry?"

She held an enormous shoe in each hand, which seemed even bigger in her hand: "Here! I bought them myself—they were on sale second-hand in our Studio, they belonged to someone's sister or brother. And I bought them, convinced they were very practical, because they were so big . . . No I can't Marina: the leather is too stiff, and they have those tops—disgusting, shining tops! And for the rest of my life! To my grave! No, I'm going to go sell them."

A few days later: "Well, Sonechka, did you sell your shoes?"

"No, Marina, they told me it was very simple: if you came there to sell—they would immediately tear the shoes away from you with their bare hands. They were indeed torn away, with their hands. But, Marina, what a torment it was—such stupid jokes, such arrogant old women and gloomy old men. And they immediately went on about the soles being like cardboard—that they weren't leather but some kind of 'raw material'. I cried, and just left. I will never try to sell anything at Smolensk market again."

And a day later, when I repeated the question: "Oh, Marina! How happy I am! I just gave them away as a gift. The girl, the landlady's daughter, was such a joy! She's twelve years old and they were just right for her. I thought about Alechka—but Alechka would have to wait six whole years—those awful people would have made her cry! But little Manka is happy, because her feet are just like that—like those shiny tops."

***

One day before her departure, I found at her house a giant young soldier, crouching politely on the edge of her quilt, his huge hands spread out on his knees: like a crab.

"And this, Marina, is my student—Senya. I'm teaching him to read."

"And is it going well?"

"Very well, he learns quickly, right, Senya?"

"Sofia Evgenievna, how do you say . . ."

"Are you reading complete syllables, or just letter by letter still?"

"Senya! (Sonechka turned purple) Listen. This is Marina Ivanovna—this citizen's name is Marina Ivanovna, she is a famous writer—Marina Tsvetaeva. Senya, please remember that! Marina Ivanovna thought I was teaching you to read the alphabet! I'm teaching him reading with expression, professional reading . . . For the two of us have known how to read for a long, long time now, right Senya?"

"It's been over a year, Sofia Evgenievna."

I will never forget the look of deep admiration when the soldier heard "the two of us . . ."

***

"Comrade, comrade" . . . No one calls me comrade on the street, and almost never—citizen, always dear citizen—and then all this right away rhymes. It's always little citizen—with something about being dark for the rhyme (although I'm not at all dark-skinned, it's just my blush that makes me look dark) or: little sweetheart, and even a whole verse:

> Dear little citizen, my pretty little cutie,
> Sit next to me and hug me on this little bench,
> Eat some little crackers with me!—

. . . and I said to him: "Where is that little cracker? It's promised—so let's see it! But dear little citizen, I'm just saying this for the song, unfortunately, I don't have any crackers, because Kolchak,[xx] the bastard, has been starving me, and if times were different—there would not only be crackers, but a whole bakery for you—for your fine sweet eyes. Because you have beautiful eyes, dear citizen." And they're all talking about my eyes, these eyes. Are they really that special? And why do only soldiers like me, and doormen in general, and even old people, and never, never—the intellectuals?

***

Many times I went on saying: "Marina . . . (Oh, Mari-ina . . . Ah, Mari-ina!)" But she had a different way of saying Marina—abrupt, with a kind of quivering in her upper lip, and inevitably preceded by something—something silly like: "M'r'n'a (like the French Marne) did you notice how he, I mean, when you said . . ." My name was already a trembling laughter, already included in the laugh, so to speak, anticipating the roll of sounds, bubbling under the lip.

My name made him sing, complain, pine, lament, and—made him laugh.

***

On the eve of her departure, she brought Alya a gift: *Childhood, Boyhood, and Youth* [by Tolstoy] in a red binding, her own childhood binding, with Seryozha Ivin's blue eyes and his broken knee, and a whole page of endearing pet names.

"Oh, Marina! I wanted to give you my *Netochka Nezvanova*[XXI] but it was stolen from me: it was borrowed and never returned. Marina! If you ever see it somewhere, buy it for yourself as a remembrance of me, everything in it is me and you, because this is our story about you and me, and the story was also never finished, like ours isn't . . ."

***

Then there was the last evening, the last song on the gramophone, the last time, the last us, the last night for the three of us, the last departure—into the last dawn.

***

A deserted square—in front of which station? It seems to me—the god-forsaken one, I don't know what—Bryansk station? Probably wooden then. Peasants and sacks, peasant women and sacks. Soldiers and sacks and still—deserted. High sun, azure sky—bluer than the dress.

We are standing there—Sonechka, me, and that soldier from the other day.

"And this, Marina, is my student!"

Coming toward us, taking on a dozen cobblestones at a time with her feet—a colossus of a woman, a young girl colossus, with a brown braid big as a fist, her blue skirt to her knees—a good meter or so to the ground, her red lacquer cheeks so red and lacquered that Sonechka's seemed pale in comparison.

And Sonechka, in response to my amazed look: "Yes, and we're only sixteen years old. And it's our first year outside the village. We want to go on stage. These are the miracles we find home in Russia!"

And then, rising on tiptoes, she stroked her lovingly.

Contrary to all likelihood, the student, still blushing, spoke in a powerful bass voice: "Sofia Evgenievna, I brought you food to take for the road. (Taking out a huge bag.) For a whole month—you'll have enough."

The train platform. Sonechka already boarded. You could hear her crying in the carriage all the way to the platform.

"Marina! Marina! Marina! Marina!"

I didn't know how to soothe her: "Sonechka, there'll be a river. And hazelnuts!"

"What do you mean, Marina? Do you take me for a squirrel with no soul? (Crying) Without you, I couldn't give a crap about any hazelnuts!

"Kiss little Alechka!

"Kiss my gramophone.

"And kiss Volodechka too."

Part Three: Sonechka's Departure

1

My precious Marina!

Despite everything, I couldn't stop—I could not keep myself from crying when I passed the very bright Povarskaya Street this morning. It will happen again, that's for sure, I will see you again and I will cry again, more often than once—but *the way* I am crying now—never, ever—

I thank you endlessly for every minute I've spent with you, and I regret the time I gave it to others—seriously, I really apologize for the fact that I once told Volodya—that he was dearest to me.

The dearest one to me is you, my Marina.

If I don't die and if I feel like going—to the autumn theater season—again, it would be only because of your love. I'd die without it—or rather, without you. Because to know that you exist is to know that Death doesn't. Could Volodya tear me away from Death with his powerful arms?

I kiss your hands a thousand times, hands that should only be kissed—though they move cabinets and lift heavy things—how immensely I love them for that.

I don't know what else to say—I have a thousand words—I have to leave. Goodbye, Marina—remember me. I know I will torment myself all summer with memories of you—Marina, Marina, what a dear name to me—who will I say it to?

Yours on this eternal, endless Journey—

Your Sonya Gollidey (I love my last name because of Irina, my dear girl).

2

I'm packed. Goodbye, my life! How many mornings have I spent on that green armchair—all alone with thoughts of you. I love everything here—because you were here.

I leave with so much heartache—because of this.

Marina—my dear, my beautiful one—I can't write, and I'm crying so senselessly.

Goodbye, my sweetheart.

Your Sonya.

3

(To Alya)

I kiss you and your little thin hands that used to hug me—I kiss you—goodbye, my Alya—I'll see you again, I'm sure.

Do a little magic so that I will have happiness and a Great Love—I feel small and not very happy.

Your Sonya.

4

June 20 (7th, old style) 1919.[I]

My dear Marina, my dear heart—I live in immense turmoil—while everyone here is whistling, singing, yelling, giggling—I can't gather my thoughts—in my heart I'm aware of my love for you, it goes everywhere with me, day and night.

I don't feel good now, Marina. The wonderful air, the forest, the larks—don't make me happy. Marina, I only knew this, felt it, and appreciated it whenever you were with me—you, Volodya, my Yurochka—even that gramophone—and I don't mean Chopin and the *Twelfth Rhapsody*—when the One I don't know yet and who I'll never meet—is with me.

Living with a heartbeat of 150 even after someone's fleeting glance (you cannot forbid them to smile!) But here I am alone—the village girls adore me, but I am lonely as a telegraph pole on the railway line. Yesterday I walked alone for a long time towards Moscow and thought: how bored they must be, so alone—after all, even telegrams are not going through anymore! Marina, I'm going to write you a trivial story, but you'll laugh and understand why I'm sad today.

Yesterday I was with Yevgeny Bagrationovich and then, for fun, I had the following exchange with a peasant woman:

Baba: Beautiful one, who are you rolling cigarettes for? Your hubby?

Sonya: Yes.

Baba: Is it the one in the white trousers?

Sonya: Yes.

Baba: Why don't you live in the same little hut with him?

Sonya: Well, he chased me away yesterday. He says I got awfully ugly, but he ordered me to roll his cigarettes—that's all I'm good for, and he took another one.

***

Evening of the same day.

The woman catches up with Vakhtangov and says:

"So why did you abandon your wife? Did you see who you exchange her for? After all, your wife is beautiful, but who did you get? Aren't you ashamed? Go back and live with your wife!"

Night of the same day.

I wash my face in the hallway. Vakhtangov enters: "Sofia Evgenievna, what's with you? Are you a child or an upstart? And what are you telling the old ladies?" And he reports what she said: I ran away from Vakhtangov, but I'm madly sorry that I'm not with him.

None of it matters. Marina, please write to me, my joy—write to me. Starting tomorrow I will move into a separate room and will keep a diary for you. My dearest. Write, I beg you, I don't understand how I can live without you. The letters are for Mr.—and for Volodya too. How is he?

Marina, they're taking my things away—I need to post this letter—don't forget me. Please, I beg you, write to me.

Oh, how I cried reading your last letter, how I love you. I kiss your precious hands, and your big stern eyes and—if it were possible, I'd kiss—your enchantingly light voice.

I live for your letters. I kiss Alechka and Irina. And my gramophone—where is everything?

Your S.

5

(The last one)

July 1 (June 20, old style) 1919.

Provincial town of Shishkovo

Marina, can you tell from what I wrote above—where I am?! The provincial town of Shishkeev—some wretched houses, huts, poor and dirty, and the forest somewhere, so hopelessly far away—I haven't been there in two weeks. I am sad and in the evenings my heart is torn with melancholy. It always seems to me that I won't live to see the morning.

At night I was writing in my diary, but now I've run out of candles, and I sit in the dark for a long time and think about you, my dear Marina. Your letter was such an unexpected joy. My God, I wept and kissed it and I kiss your beloved hands that wrote it.

Marina, when I die, write these lines of yours on my cross:

. . . Everything ended with the refrain:

My dear little one!

Such an amazing poem.

Marina, my heart, I write so incoherently. Today is so blue and so hot—everything is so noisy that I can't even think. I'm writing in a mad hurry, since Vakhtang Levanovich is leaving for Moscow—and I have only a half an hour to finish. Marina, I beg you, my heart, my Life—Marina!—don't leave for the Crimea yet, not until August 1st. I'll arrive by the 1st, I'll die if I don't see you—I'll have nothing to live for if I don't see you then.

Marina, my beloved, my golden one, don't leave—I don't know what else to say.

I love you more than anyone and everything and—no matter what I say—through it all.

Marina, sweet one, gentle one, dear one, I kiss you, your eyes, hands. I kiss Alechka and her hands for writing the letter. I despise the father, the son and his detestable love for "a certain married princess"—I'm upset Volodya doesn't write, truly upset.

My sweetheart, Marina, do not forget me.

Your Sonya.

I'm writing a diary for you.

On the way to Ruzaevka, I sent Volodya a telegram at one of the stations:

I kiss you—across hundreds of

Disconnected miles!

I gave it to the telegraph operator, but he didn't want to accept it as a telegram, it wasn't urgent he said—it's not done. I had a lot of trouble convincing him.

I kiss you.

I'm praying for you.

Sonya.

P.S. There is a church opposite my house, I go to matins and cry.

***

After Sonechka's departure, I had the weakness to go looking for her—tracing her steps. I suddenly forced myself to believe that there was nothing extraordinary about her—that there were people around like her.

But, much to my surprise, I soon discovered that Sonechka, nevertheless—was no longer—as if, I mean the same as if when you don't have any cigarettes left, you mechanically stuffed anything into your mouth—anything, a pencil, a toothbrush. You feel bad. You calm down for a while, and then, still feeling unwell, you notice that you picked up the wrong thing.

After my love for Sonechka, the studio people seemed to accept me with great affection, quite warmly. One studio member even suggested that when Irina returned from the countryside, she'd take her to another village . . . I had seen her a few times—but—she also had brown hair and blue eyes—soon it became clear that Sonechka had nothing to do with this. She simply became a friend. A new and different friend of mine.

As in a book—"to be continued"—yet here there was no continuation.

***

The sequel—our sequel—was being realized with Volodya, what we were before Sonechka, not the way we separated or were brought together by her. It seemed natural: after the disappearance of her tiny physical presence between us, we could fill her tiny physical absence with ourselves and lean slightly closer to one another, that is to say, simply sit next to each other, simply find ourselves side by side. Not by agreement—but as if we had agreed in advance, not using her disappearance as an excuse. We separated and sat down he—in his remote corner, and I—on my distant edge, at a distance from each other of a good one and a half times Sonechka. That little dark head between us had disappeared and did not bring our heads closer together. As if everything we'd experienced with Sonechka had been only a dream and was only possible with Sonechka, and only in dreams.

But here I must name someone else: Martin Eden.

There is a great deal to be said: an object, a hero, and author all in one. More than I can say myself. Someday, when we part . . . Marina Ivanovna, read *Martin Eden*, and when you reach the place where the blond-haired rider arrives on a white horse—remember me and understand me . . .

Nineteen years later, nineteen and a half years later, in November 1937, walking in Paris in the rain, I passed an unfamiliar street. I was with my Russian companion Kolya—who was a little older than my Volodya at that time.

"Marina Ivanovna! Maybe you'd like to look at these old books—in the rain."

I picked up the tarpaulin slightly: *Martin Eden* stares up at me.

Now—an explanation. It would be crazy to think that I, who live only on dreams and memories, could have forgotten Volodya's wish.

But it wasn't so easy to walk into a shop and ask for *Martin Eden*.

Just as Volodya once came into my life—on his own, like everything great in my life which also came on its own—or did not come at all, so *Martin Eden* had to come into my life alone.

That's how he came that day—in the rain, because of a random word from my companion.

He stood before me.

All I could do was reach out my hand—to him, soaked in the rain, dying from the indifference of passersby. (Let us recall the end of *Martin Eden* and of Jack London himself!)

In this respectable bookshop—a new *Martin Eden*, with pages still uncut, any *Martin Eden*, any copy of *Martin Eden*—would have been a betrayal of Volodya, a triple betrayal: Jack London, Martin Eden and Volodya. All their lives they struggled against the establishment. They even gave their lives in sacrifice.

And so—in the rain, from under the modest tarpaulin, at the last minute before closing, from the hands of an indifferent merchant—it was a kind of salvation: from Martin Eden and from the memory of Volodya himself. There Martin Eden needed me, I extended a helping hand to him, I truly pulled him out of trouble with my hand.

And so, at the end of this amazing book—was that blonde horseman. I didn't look for him either, didn't even wait, knowing full well he would appear—in his own time in the book! At the end of this paean to the solitude of labor and growing up, this paean to *solitude* at the twelfth hour of his existence in the world . . .

. . . a vision not of a rider, but of a white rower, a swimmer, a white-faced wild man of the Pacific, standing on a tree trunk, in whom I recognized that other blond horseman (who never existed, but was only in my memory)—I recognized him.

Nineteen years later, Martin Eden validated Volodya for me.

***

One day when I was reading to him from my notebook. Zavadsky, Pavlik, Sonechka, myself, conversations in the queues one after another, reflections, etc.—he said, with a playful bitterness:

"Marina Ivanova, but I'm still a little offended—why is there nothing about me? About us? About what belongs to us?"

"You know, I am not envious of you in the external world, in life, but in the world of thought—how can I put it? I myself never wrote anything down, in fact, I have a child's handwriting—I know that everything is eternal, in me—everything is eternal, everything will remain and at the right time—it will all surface. Everything, every word of ours, I even feel that by writing something down it would be insulting, belittling. But you are different, you are a writer . . ."

"Have you ever noticed this Volodya, even once during our entire friendship?"

He grinned: "Others have told me . . ."

"Stop, Volodya! I have two lines of poetry about you, poems never end:

If God made you tsar,

You'd be given the nickname—Gentle One.

I can see with my own eyes how he lets the lines sink into his heart and that's where he listens to them. With a hint of a mocking smile:

"Marina Ivanova. It's only with you—I am so gentle."

***

I have not yet mentioned his smile: rare, brief, confusing, very modest, almost as if he is ashamed, with downcast eyes—looking down and even condescendingly to those around him, but never looking at me, whenever I began to talk about Zavadsky. A smile that almost forcibly brought together his lips ready to part, bringing them back to their original place—of non-laughter. It's strange but true, I ask that it be verified: such a smile occurs in two-year-old children who still speak very little—they invariably look away and sometimes completely close their eyes. Yes, Volodya had a child's smile, provided you let go of all the commonplaces associated with a childhood.

And yet—such a smile (of silent accomplishment and obvious discomfort) is also found on the faces of very young fathers—over their first-born child: necessarily a son. If there was discomfort in the hard-to-put-together lips, there was superiority in the eyes.

Volodya, Volodya, wherever I am, if I see on someone's face the *beginning* of this smile—whether on a two-year-old child in a park, or a forty-year-old English captain in a film—there would be no park, no film, no child, no captain—if it didn't end in your smile.

And everything would be as it was then.

***

He and I never talked about Sonechka. I knew that he loved her in a different way than I did, and she loved him in a different way than she did me, that both of us together wouldn't agree with her, that for him she was less than what she was in reality—because she was everything that she had given to me, and one cannot be whole with two separate people—you can't be everything at once. One can only be whole with the two people together, that is, the three of us, our own threesome, was now over.

I don't even know if he ever wrote to her.

A conversation about her would certainly end in disagreement, I felt that he did not have the key to understanding her; and to tell the truth, he was too young for her, too young for her childishness, beneath which, at the height of his twenty years, he could not guess all her troubles or all the unhappiness of his destiny. For him to love was to pray, how could one pray before such a small person, even if you knelt down, one would inevitably feel taller and older?

Our gramophone even fell silent, it turned out to be only Sonechka's voice—that second parallel voice, whose absence she so often and so bitterly deplored in her own heart.

Sonechka, her gramophone, her green armchair, her unsold yellow shoes, her Yura, her Volodya, and even her Marina—all of her and all of herself. With her in my heart, I—transported myself into the future, to the day of our new meeting in which I firmly believed.

And all those days without her—it was as if I'd remained standing, protecting my eyes from the sun with my hand, like a peasant woman in the field waiting—"can't you see anyone coming?" Or as if sleeping like a little girl who was promised a new doll—now she sleeps, she never stops sleeping, and she gets up asleep, she goes to bed, still sleepy—she sleeps thinking, so that time would pass quickly! Or like a prisoner who counts the days by crossing them out on the wall, one stick and then another. Just like when one goes to meet someone—so I lived to meet her, to see her—with every step I took, with every moment of the day, with each thought in my head—just like she did, then, along the railway, going towards Moscow, that is—towards me.

Oh, no I didn't miss her at all—because I was so happy with her!

Here are some echoes of her in my notebook of those days:

> Immediately before me I see Alya's knees and long legs. She is lying on the roof, with her legs dangling over the windowsill: Marina! Look! A cloud is floating by—maybe it's your mother's soul? Marina, maybe at this moment the Little Mermaid is approaching our house—the one who was three hundred years old? (She crosses herself when she hears music from the street.) Marina! Marina! Marina! There is the smoke. My God! After all, the smoke is flying

everywhere, everywhere! Marina, maybe it's smoke from the train that Sonechka is traveling on? Marina, maybe this is smoke from Joan of Arc's fire? How many souls have come up to this height?

***

"I won't say anything about the women, because I remember them all with great gratitude, but really I only love Sonechka Gollidey."

***

When I think about Sonechka Gollidey's arrival, I can't believe it: never was there such happiness.

I think about her—and I leave out the essentials. Like a new ring, like a pink dress, no matter how ridiculous it looks: there's passionate desire.

For it's not Sonechka who's going to arrive, but Love itself.

***

I dream of Sonechka Gollidey like a lump of sugar: guaranteed sweetness.

***

(Even if my whole story is like a lump of sugar, at least I felt sweetness in writing it!)

***

"Marina Ivanovna! Today is our last evening. Tomorrow I'm leaving for the south."

"The last . . . tomorrow . . . But why didn't you, couldn't you, let me know earlier . . ."

"Marina Ivanovna!"—her voice is so serious it sounds threatening. "Don't make me say what I shouldn't say and what you shouldn't hear. Rest assured I had serious reasons."

"Hiding it from me is the worst? To walk to my house as if nothing happened, but to find out yourself? To know all by yourself?"

"W-well, if you really want to know about my . . ."

"What? This or that, it's simply this—I don't want anything. Go with God, just go wherever you please! I just—I dreamed about all this—if you want—just dreamed about it—once again—I dreamed all this!"

"Marina Ivanovna! After all, you are a human being, and I am one too, and to be a person is to suffer. Why should I, to whom you gave so much joy, only joy, cause you suffering before I go? My own was enough."

"Volodya, have you really made up your mind?"

"My suitcase is packed."

"Are you going alone?"

"No, there are several of us. Several studio members. I'll part from them later."

"Do I understand you correctly?"

"Yes."

"And your parents?"

"They think it's about acting. Everyone thinks—it's for acting. There's only you, Marina Ivanovna, there's nothing else here for me. This is not life. There's no life for me here. I cannot act at life while others live it. Act while other people die. I'm not an actor."

"I always knew that."

"Now let's forget about everything and spend the evening as always."

And the evening passed—as every other evening passed—like every other time.

***

Suddenly when seeing him—a veil was lifted from my eyes!

"But the Angel—it was you, Volodechka!"

"What? (he understood, and got self-conscious:)—Oh, you're talking about . . . (now firmly:)—No, Marina Ivanovna, I'm not an angel: my greatest dream is to one day become a human being."

Then, in the same voice, not his own: the one for Sonechka, the dreamy, sleepy one, as if to himself, not to me:

"Maybe I was too honest . . ."

And, later:

"Charlemagne—maybe not Charlemagne—once said: You must speak to God in Latin, and to the enemy—in German, to a woman—in French . . . (Silence.) And so—there you are—it seems I speak with women in Latin . . ."

***

(I didn't hug him then, but that wasn't what he wanted from me—and it's not what he wanted with me . . .)

***

Just before he left, he was still in the room—it was already getting light:

"Marina Ivanovna, you always liked my ring. Take it! When we first met, I wanted to give it to you, and then—almost every time we saw each other, but I was always waiting for something. Now that something has come. It's not a gift, Marina Ivanovna, it's a tribute."

"Volodya! It's the first time someone has given me a ring, it's always me giving, and (I took it and held it up). If I haven't given you one till now, it's only because I've given one to Yuri Z. and to Pavlik, and to many others! I just didn't want, I couldn't, let you be—I mean—in that lineup."

"How I envied them! Now I can say to Pavlik and Zavadsky—that this one is from *your* hand—and so solid! Actually (laughing)—I was simply dying with envy! No, Marina Ivanovna, you must give it to me, and I won't be in that lineup, at the Studio, yes—I would have been standing in the line, where I am going, too . . . Even so, I *could*—stand in that line—I wouldn't be offended."

With admiration:

"And the seal is all set to engrave my name. I'm so used to seeing it on your hand that now I'll feel like my hand is yours. (Holding it at a distance)—Zavadsky's is smaller. His is from a Chinese woman, but mine is from a Chinese man, a Chinese sage."

"From the simplest coolie, Volodechka."

"And if he's a coolie on top of that, then the whole social question is solved!"

We joke like this, but the melancholy mounts and mounts . . .

"Volodya, do you know why poets exist? In order not to be ashamed to say the greatest things:

My roads will always safeguard—
The imprint of you.

We stand under my poplars, once barely green and now silvery, so silvery that neither branches nor trunk are visible.

"No, no, Marina Ivanovna, don't think this is the last time, I'll come back tomorrow, that is, today, I'll come again today—for the children's pictures—and to truly say goodbye."

***

When he came the next day, seeing him for the first time in the sunlight, ever since our first and only daytime walk, a century ago—I was amazed:

"Volodya! What is this? You're not dark-haired at all! Your hair is chestnut!"

"Yes, light brown, Marina Ivanovna."

"Lord, I've been friends with a dark-haired man for a whole year and a half!"

"Perhaps you'll also say that my eyes are dark?"—he said, a little sad.

"No, they're blue-gray, I always knew that, I was friends with the gray ones . . . But your hair is a kind of dream!"

"Marina Ivanovna, I'm afraid," there's bitterness in his voice under the layer of jokes, "that you saw everything about me in your own way! All of me, and not only (a contemptuous wave at his hair)—this!"

"And if I did—is it wrong?"

"No, Marina Ivanovna, it was good, even too good, that's why I'm afraid of being in the daylight with you. Now I'm brown-haired, but tomorrow I might turn out to be boring. Maybe it's good that I'm going?"

"Volodya! Don't drive me crazy, my patience with you has worn thin, worn thin! Because you yourself are never satisfied—and maybe you won't leave! I have so much on my plate, right now—I'm going to lose it!"

"No need, Marina Ivanovna, you mustn't."

***

We were sitting in the attic room where Alya used to climb up to the roof to meet me.

"Alechka! I have a request for you: read your mama's poems to me!"

"Right away, Volodechka!"

She came running over with a crimson book, which she kept in the kitchen under her pillow.

Your gray donkey clops straight ahead,
Unafraid of the woods or the river . . .
Dear kind Christmas Lady,
Take me with you to the clouds!
I will bring bread for your donkey . . .

The little voice whispered . . .

***

"Marina Ivanovna, I brought you a gift! You know what my favorite book is about—Joan of Arc? Do you know it? By Mark Twain—it's wonderful."

I open it: a dedication. I close it, without reading it.

"Marina Ivanovna, I've always boasted about having a personal armory, a museum, a library of my own—I never showed it to anyone, because this is what was there: a Spanish pistol, my ring and two books: *Martin Eden* and this book. Now you have my entire arsenal—my entire museum—and my entire library. I'm clean."

"Marina! (Alya's voice.) Can I give Volodechka my *Magic Lantern*?[II] So he can read it in the carriage if the soldiers get too rude. He can read it to them, because the surprise will calm them down and they'll fall asleep. Peasants always fall asleep hearing poetry. When I read poetry to Nadya, she always fell asleep."

Volodya kissed her hand and took the book she held: "I'm not going with soldiers, Alechka, I'm going with crazy people, they say they are calm, but these days none of them are quiet, they're all furious."

"Then I don't think they'll fall asleep hearing Marina's poems!"

***

"Volodya, Marina and I have written letters for you to read on the way, just as we once wrote for Papa to read on the train. These are our farewell voices."

***

"What time is your train?"

"I have to go soon."

"How about if we go with you and see you off?"

"No, Marina Ivanovna, I want to say goodbye to you—here."

***

"Now let's sit down a few moments before leaving."[III]

We sit in a row on the narrow mahogany sofa. Alya prays out loud: "May God grant Volodya a happy journey and let him find in the South what he is looking for. And then return to Moscow—on a white horse. Also that we will still be alive, with our house still standing. Amen."

We cross ourselves, get up, and go down the narrow mezzanine staircase into the endless darkness of the corridor. Faced with my usual urge—to go further and walk out with him:

"Don't go any further with me. It'll be a long walk."

The very last moment. Should I tell him or not? Will he say something or . . .

Then, as if he'd been doing it all his life, he embraces my head, presses me to his chest, kisses my head, kisses my forehead, my lips.

Then I bless him three times, first I make a cross over his forehead, then shoulders, then his chest, the cruciform design of his face.

He has taken a step back: already beyond the threshold, not holding out his hand over the threshold,[IV] of course: "Farewell, Marina (swallowing a mountain)—Ivanovna."

***

Dear Volodya!

I hope it's not too stuffy in the train car, and you are given food there, and treated well, and no one bothers you, and you get an open window. I want the whole journey to be as pleasant and exhilarating as it was before. You are leaving, our last true friend.

Volodya, I just raised my head and was ready to start crying. I'm very sad. You were the last one who truly loved us, and were so gentle with us, and loved listening to poetry too. You have Marina's children's book. When you read it, remember how I used to read it to you. Soon someone will go to Kyiv again and we'll send letters to you again.

Volodya. It doesn't seem real to me that you won't be here. Oh my God! These train cars will not be set on fire since all the passengers are innocent. Try to stay invisible and come up with a good disease for yourself. Something terrible could happen . . .

The horrors that were supposed accompany Volodya's journey, according to Alya, did not make it into the letter, because Volodya's farewell knock was suddenly heard, and I did not have time to finish copying her words into my notebook. What Alya wrote next was a description of Volodya being placed in the train to Kyiv, like the most dangerous of madmen.

***

The Joan of Arc book bore the inscription: "You and I, we love—the same thing."

***

Then a letter, just one, with only several lines.

The letter ended with the words: I firmly hope that we will meet again. This belief will stay alive.

Then began—the silence.

***

There was a knock at the door. I opened it—Sonechka.

Bliss? No. A blow—so strong I could barely stand on my feet.

And in my ears—the familiar stream of words: "Marina . . . and something else, Mar-, something again, and then again: Mar-rina . . . and only little by little, and words emerged from the stream: "Only an hour, only one hour, I have only one hour. I only have one hour left with you. I just arrived and now I'm leaving again . . . We only have one hour left! I came to see you. Only one hour."

We passed some tenants going down the stairs.

Sonechka turned to them: "I'm Sofia Evgenievna Gollidey, I have a couple of things to say to you."

The father and son obediently came back up. We all stood on the landing.

"You are wicked people! How can you exploit a single woman like this, alone, without a husband, and with two small children?!"

"But we . . . we . . ."

"You burst into the kitchen while she was sleeping to wash yourself (splashing around like three cats) under a running stream! As if that makes you cleaner! You sold her watch but didn't give her any money! You were in her room, where she keeps her books and notebooks, hanging up your dirty, dirty laundry!"

"But—excuse me . . . Sofia Evgenievna?" said the younger one, offended. "We only hung out our wet, clean things!"

"Well, clean is still ugly. Because there is an attic with beams, but you are too lazy to climb up there."

"But the floor is collapsing in there, and the beams will fall on your head . . ."

"It's fine if it collapses . . . and fine if they fall . . ."

"And, actually, Marina Ivanovna rented this room out to us."

"But you never paid her."

"It's because we don't have any money now: we're not giving it up."

"You know, this is so unfair, your whole attitude towards Marina is unfair. Even criminal. Didn't you wake her up in the middle of the night when the whole yard was full of soldiers? And didn't you slip her some idiotic memoirs and portraits under the door—and even some kind of Maltese sword?"

"But Marina Ivanovna She herself said that if . . ."

"I know that. And you took advantage of her. What if she had been shot?"

(The father was silent and breathed heavily, basically agreeing with all of it.)

"Remember: I'm leaving now. But I'll be back. And if I find out that you—do you understand me? There will be big trouble—illness—and typhoid, and scabies, and whatever—I will simply curse you."

(It must be said that after this the Poles calmed down a little, and when the first cold weather came they moved out. I will add that they were not bad people, but I was a big fool.)

***

We were sitting upstairs, on Volodya's sofa, saying goodbye. The room was slanting with rays of tears.

"Marina, I feel very strange—as if I'd already died and am revisiting different places—Marina, is the gramophone still playing?"

"I haven't started it up since then, Sonechka."

"And Volodechka is gone. It's not that he's not here—he's often not here—he's not going to come in . . . Hasn't it only been a week since he left? It's a pity . . .

"If I knew everything would be so terrible, perhaps I would never have come to visit you the first time?"

"Was this the part where the cat climbed into your window? Every night—at what time? Marina, maybe it was my death—he smelled of valerian, didn't he?—when you die, it also smells like ether . . . Because why did he have to climb in, when there was nothing to eat? He came for me, Marina, for our death, for the end of it all . . . So pale and light gray, almost completely invisible—like the dawn? And covered in drool? Oh, how disgusting, Marina, how disgusting! Well, of course, it was not a cat, Marina—just your humility . . . And during these hours I did not sleep and cried, cried terribly, Marina, for you, and for me . . .

". . . Marina, if you ever find out that I have women friends, a woman friend, don't believe it: it's all because of my eternal fear of solitude, a terrible weakness that you never wanted to see in me.

"Or—if you hear of a man—please don't believe it. Because it is always in a fog—pitiful—in reality a disregard of myself.

"It was you I've loved, in my sound mind and clearest memory—it was you alone, I loved you madly.

"This, Marina, is my legacy."

***

". . . I bequeath to you—Yura, he is not as insignificant as he seems *to us*, not really so heartless . . . I don't know if he's in the city now, I only had an hour with him, and the hour was yours—and I didn't dare ask you . . . Marina! I don't dare ask you, I beg you: don't abandon Yura! Think of him with kindness—at least think about him . . . And if you see him in winter (of course, I'll return in the Fall), tell him, but not directly—for he doesn't like—oh well, you know!—tell him even if I get married, he's still my favorite angel, of all the angels . . ."

I would have loved Volodya like this all my life, loved him all my life, but he could not love me—he could only kiss me—and even then (with a little smile) somewhat reluctantly and with effort. That's why he kissed me so hard.

Do you think he'll ever come back?

***

". . . And my Alechka isn't here . . . Tell her when she returns from her Krylatskoye [Winged Village] (what a name!) that it's a daughter like her I would have loved to have, a daughter like her—but I know I never will never have one.

"Why, Marina, did I have to love everything about you, even down to the last cobweb in my house, every last crack in the house? Only to lose everything?

". . . What time is it now? Oh, it's in—your *Adventures*[V]—when she keeps asking: what time is it? And then again: what time is it? She never hears the answer, because it's not what time is it, but: when is—death? Marina, can't we go back in time and turn everything in our hands—like a river? Make it flow backwards? So that it would be winter again—and that scene—when you are reading from *Blizzard*. Let it not be the last time, but make it the first time?

"Oh, if only someone had told me it would all end like this! Not only would I never have come to you the first time, but I would have refused to come into the world...

"But again, what time is it, Marina? I'm asking you—seriously. Because they wouldn't let me come to your house, I begged and pleaded, gave my word of honor that I would be at the station at four sharp . . .

"Marina, why am I leaving? After all, it wouldn't kill anyone if I didn't leave? After all, no one would die? Marina, do you understand? I am now leaving you, when you mean everything to me—because I gave my word to be at the station at four. And at the station—why? Who made all this happen?

"No, Marina, there's no need to say anything—there's no time. (What time is it, Marina?) It was—is and ever will be without you, as it was always:—*non-being,* non-existence, there was nothing. Now (crying bitterly) for the first time this entire month—I'm living, this last hour before my death—I am alive for however long I have left to live, Marina— this will be my last hour."

We get up, we get up to go. She stops at the kitchen threshold:

"And my Irina is not here either. I knew she was gone, but somehow I wasn't expecting an empty crib . . . (she seemed distraught:) Gally-da, Gally-da . . .

"Marina, I want to come to your room—say goodbye to the lantern, to the gramophone . . . Oh, I forgot—the Poles are there with their 'wet and clean' underwear . . .

"Marina! Don't come with me! Even down to the first landing! Let it be the same as the first time I came to you: I was on the other side of the threshold, and you were on the inside, and there was your beloved face in the darkness of the corridor.

"I'm going with the "second batch" (laughing through her tears)—like a convict! Son'ka the convict. Sonya is a convict. I can't stay with them after being with you! I'll kill them or throw myself out of the window! (Quietly, almost whispering:)

To leave feeling lovesickness
How can I go on the iron railway?
The locomotive sputter and sputter,
And with its gloomy sound
I will think and think that
The devil has taken me away . . .

"Marina! How awful it is—what's happening! Because it's the devil himself who is taking me away from you . . ."

Her last words ring in my ears:

"Marina! I'll be back in the fall! I'll be back in the fall!"

***

"So, have you seen your Sonechka?"

"Sonechka? When?"

"What do you mean—when? Well, yesterday, of course. Didn't she leave yesterday again? Didn't she stop by your house? She's so unfaithful!"

I don't know why but I suddenly had the impression that my room had aged . . . The walls and floors had faded, everything had become dull; there were even more cobwebs. I don't know why, but when I looked out the window, it seemed to me that the house opposite had also sagged and tarnished in turn, that the plaster on the columns was peeling and crumbling, and the cornices turning black and cracking, and the walls were turning from dark yellow to piebald.

Or was it a ray of sunshine, suddenly peeking out from behind a cloud that hid again under a rain cloud? And everything became more decrepit in my eyes, or perhaps the whole prospect of my future flashing before me appeared so hostile and sad, and I saw myself as I would be now, exactly fifteen years later, aged, in the same room, and still just as alone . . . [from *White Nights*]

***

After this first blow, which I parried—a stone to my exposed breast, and a mortal coldness of my heart and immortal coldness of my forehead—like Caesar said (nothing to laugh about!)—And you, Brutus?—I don't hear the reproach, only—regret, condescension: as if Brutus were lying down and Caesar leaning over him . . .

But let's keep it short and simple: I didn't understand, but I accepted it—precisely as one accepts a blow: because one is a body, and this body happened to be in the way.

Before my departure from Russia—in April of 1922, that is, for three whole years, I did not make a single attempt to find Sonechka; after three years of coexistence with her in the same country, I basically thought of her as dead: deceased. And this was the message from the first moment of the news to the last syllable of the sentence: she came and she left.

"I want to remember my offense, Nastenka?" [from *White Nights*]

There was no offense.

I *knew* that her not coming—was an act, her absence—was imagined. Can someone who accompanies you, like the blood in your veins, *be absent*, she who can feel your heart's blood sooner than she can see the light?

And if at first I seemed to be a little angry, indignant, it was only on the surface—the surface of the actions, hoping that with this indignation everything would turn ordinary: reverse fate. (If I got angry and offended at Sonechka, that meant she existed.)

But not for a second did I believe in the depths of my soul that for some reason she wouldn't come, but just like that, she didn't come, she did not come.

And the more people sympathized with me: "her ungratefulness, frivolity, infidelity"—the more lonely I felt and the more deeply I understood.

I knew we had to part. If I had been a man, it would have been my happiest love—whereas here—we inevitably had to part, because her love for me would inevitably have gotten in the way—had already gotten in the way—of her loving another, always in the shadows, the one whom she always would have betrayed me with, just as she inevitably betrayed both Yura and Volodya.

It was absolutely necessary for her to tear herself away from me—her very flesh and soul, both hers and mine.

***

Sonechka abandoned me—to fulfill her destiny as a woman. Her not coming back to me was simply obedience to her vocation as a woman: to love a man—in the end, it didn't matter which man—and to love only him—until death.

None of the commandments included—me, my love for her, her love for me, our love. They don't sing about her and me in church and don't speak of us in the Gospel.

Her departure from me was a simple and honest fulfillment of the words of the Apostle: "And a man will leave his father and his mother . . ." I was undoubtedly more than father and mother to her, more than her beloved, but she was obliged to prefer him, this stranger, to me. Because this is how God created the world.

Both of us only went against people: never against God and never against human beings.

***

But how could I reconcile that feeling of joyful possession of Sonechka, the concrete and inseparable that Sonechka was for me, this feeling of a ring on my finger—how can I reconcile that with the drooping arms that let go, and that fell away from me?

There you have it—I could only really lose it so completely after having possessed it so . . .

Reader, remember?—"or all at once with the finger . . ."

Sonechka was torn away from me—along with my heart.

***

When death comes along an intelligent animal knows immediately: that's it!—and stops treating itself with herbs and remedies. I am an intelligent animal—and I can immediately recognize my death, and rejecting all the herbs and remedies, I accept it. No: it was not Sonechka who died for me, nor was it love that died—Sonechka died in my life, that is, she entirely went inside, into that mountain, into the cave where she so prophetically was afraid of disappearing—into the abyss.

For the whole miracle I experienced with her was—that she was outside of me, and not inside of me, she was not a projection of my dreams or my longing, but an independent thing, beyond my imagination, beyond my conjecture. I did not dream her, did not sing her. The miracle was she was not in my heart but in my room. That for once in my life not only did I add nothing, but—I was almost overwhelmed by everything, that is to say, I received the full measure of everything I had taken and given.

***

Sonechka was given to me—so I could hold her for a time—in my hands, in my arms. A child did not become mine when I held him in my arms for a time. My hands were just as empty, after holding the child.

Every child we hold like this is taken away from us by—their mother. Sonechka's mother was—destiny.

***

Was it hurtful? A betrayal?

Sonechka's failure to arrive for the last time was the same as Volodya's coming—for the last time—it had the same weight: the weight of his entire being. And it meant exactly the same thing.

Just as Volodya came, she never came, and with her entire being she did not come just as he did.

Sonechka's refusal to come to me was—an act of love.

It was the first step of her absence from my life, the first hour of her silent otherworldly presence in me—settling into me from beyond.

Sonechka did not come to me, because she would have died, she would have simply dissolved in her tears, there would be nothing left of Sonechka—but a puddle. Or her heart would have stopped at the last syllable of my name.

Volodya came because he couldn't leave me without saying goodbye, Sonechka didn't come because she couldn't say goodbye.

But there was yet another reason she didn't come: Sonechka didn't come—because she was already dead.

This way of not coming—belongs only to the dead, they can't because the earth holds them. And for a long, long time I felt her close to me, almost within the reach of my hand, exactly the same way one feels a dead person, on whose hand one doesn't close one's hand, solely because it shouldn't be done and because it would upset all known laws: equal fears—encountering the void and encountering the hand.

In the end—I only stopped hearing Sonechka or seeing her.

***

Give us this day our daily bread . . .

No, she has never been my daily bread: who am I, that she could be my daily bread? My humility would never have allowed this. Not our daily bread, not essential bread, but a miracle—there is no such prayer: Give us our essential miracle today. There was neither the weight of our daily bread in her, nor its firm necessity, nor its fate, nor our condemnation, nothing to do with—by the sweat of your brow . . . Could I win Sonechka as a daily wage? For a lifetime of labor? No, such a life can only be offered as a gift.

Like Cordelia, in the Shakespeare of my youth, says in King Lear—my salt. For me Sonechka—was indispensable as sugar, with the same humility: I needed her—like sugar. As everyone knows, sugar is not necessary, you can live without it. For four years of the Revolution we did well without it, replacing it with molasses at times, and at other times with grated beetroot, sometimes with saccharin and sometimes with nothing at all. We drank plain tea. We didn't die. But we didn't live either.

Without salt, we fell ill with scurvy, without sugar there was: grief.

A whole lump of white sugar, alive—that's what Sonechka was to me.

Is it harsh? Yes, brutal—like Cordelia: I love you like salt, no more, no less. You can love the old king like salt, but . . . a little girl? No, enough salt. Let it be said once in a lifetime: I loved her as one loved sugar during the Revolution. And that's all there is to it.

***

Can you say it right now?
Last longer
You are so beautiful . . . [Goethe]

No, I didn't have that with her. There was something else—the opposite and greater:

God bless! It would have been beautiful
God bless! Fate did not will it!

A great poetic conditional: *would*, the one and only poetic possessive: *would.*

There was fate. And as they say in Russian: it was non-fate (not written).

***

Let us remember the words of King David: God granted man seventy years, anything more is divine mercy.

Three months were granted to us, to Sonechka and me. No, *all* of Sonechka , an eternity of three months I had with her—it was already *more* than a human life and heart.

Maria . . . Miranda . . . Mireill. All she had to do was be herself, and she was all the others, too.

Thus the prophetic words of forgetful Pavlik were fulfilled in her:

The one with many names . . .

The was true for me, too, but it was not only names that took on her face.

All the male lyric poetry up to that time was without an object or with an object—opposite to the poet himself. I could not be the heroine of the poet's love, or insert myself into this, or put my face into it as in a mirror. I couldn't. I wanted to love myself and I was a poet myself. All male lyric poetry acquired a face: Sonechka's. All the voids of "you," of "she"—which in all languages expresses the overflow of a poet's heart and the fullness of his self suddenly came to life and were filled with her face. In the oval void, in the round zero of every female image reflected in a poet's lines, Sonechka's face found itself framed as in a medallion.

But no, Nicolas Lenau[VI] writes it better—vaster!

The forest roars, the sky
Flies in the storm's thunderclaps
I paint it into the weather
Oh little one! Your face . . .

The songs of all nations speak of Sonechka, every barbarian under the moon celebrates Sonechka. For the Kyrgyz—it's Sonechka, the Tahitian—it's Sonechka, all of Goethe, all of Lenau, all the longing of all poets is about Sonechka, all the embraces—for Sonechka, all the separations—are from Sonechka . . .

Needless to say that after her I have never loved another female creature and, of course, never will love, for I love less and less. I'll save all the remaining ardor for those whom she can no longer warm.

***

Winter of 1919-1920. There's no more knocking on the door because it no longer closes: someone has broken the lock. So, instead of a knock on the door, there's the sound of boots shaking off snow and a voice from downstairs:

"Is this where Marina Ivanovna Tsvetaeva lives?"

"Yes. Please come up the stairs."

He comes in. A stranger. Young. I know I've never seen this man. I also know one more thing: the one who came in is an enemy.

"I am Alexey, brother of Volodya Alexeyev. Have you heard from my brother?"

"I did. A long time ago. One letter. Around the same time."

"We never got anything."

"It was just a few words: that he hoped to see me again, he was in good health . . ."

"And since then?"

"Nothing."

"Can I ask you a question? And excuse me in advance. What kind of relationship did you have with my brother? I'm asking you because—we were very close, that's all. He related to the whole family—he left last Easter—he left and went to your house, and (swallowing with difficulty, like Volodya) he spent his last evening with you . . . Are you a friend? A lover? An affair?"

"It was love."

"What do you mean?"

"Just what I said. I won't add another word."

(He fell silent, not taking his eyes off me, I didn't raise mine.)

I said: "Give me your address just in case . . ."

"Don't you know our address?"

"No, Volodya always came to my house, I didn't write to him . . ."

"And you knew nothing about us, his father, mother, brothers?"

"I knew there was a family. And that he loved them."

"So what kind of attitude is this . . . anti-social?" (We fell silent.)

"It means—you never loved him? That's what I thought—because you don't leave a woman you love—and who loves you . . ."

"Think whatever you want, but one thing is true—and tell your parents: I never hurt him—ever."

"This is all very strange, besides, he is an actor, and you are a writer . . . Please forgive me. I was harsh, I couldn't control myself, I didn't expect this . . . I know you're not supposed to talk to women like that, you were very kind to me, you could have just thrown me out the door. But if you only knew what kind of grief there was at home. Do you have any idea if he's alive?"

"Yes, he is."

"But why doesn't he write? Even to you?"

"He has written to you many times—but letters don't arrive."

"And you don't think he's dead?"

"My God!—certainly not."

"I'll tell my parents that. I'll tell them you are sure—thank God!—(a big sign of the cross)—he's alive—and that he is writing letters—and that . . . Now I'll go. Have you forgiven me?"

"No, I wasn't offended."

And at the door, he said: "How do you live like this without locking yourself in? And you don't you lock yourself in at night either? And what a strange apartment you have: dark and huge with all sorts of strange passages . . . Will you allow me to visit you from time to time?"

"I would be very happy to see you."

"Well, good. God bless you!"

"And God bless you!"

***

He never came back.

***

Finally, about Yuri. Just before my departure from Russia, it was already April 1922. I met him on a large wide stone staircase in some institutional office where I went to get some papers, I met him there for the last time. He was going downstairs, and I was going up. There was a second's delay, a moment of awkwardness—I looked at him in silence, as always, and like before: from bottom to top. Again we were on the stairs! The face looked like that of a hunted man, like a large bird that had just been caught, struggling: "Don't think, I mean, you didn't understand . . . you misunderstood . . . all this is so complicated . . . And it's so far from simple . . ."

"Yes, yes, of course, I know, I've known for a long time . . . Farewell, Yuri Alexandrovich, farewell forever. I'm leaving one of these days—I'm leaving forever . . ."

And I went up, and he went down. And we were separated.

In a few words, this is what happened to the characters in this story:

Pavlik A.—is married, has two daughters (one of them a beauty—in memory of Sonechka?). He is publishing.

Yuri Z.—is married, has a son and acts.

His sister Verochka, I later met in Paris. About her I need to write a separate story. She died in 1930 of tuberculosis in Yalta. The day before her death she wrote me her last postcard in pencil: "Marina! My grief at not seeing you is as enormous as this elephant."

. . . They were brother and sister, and they had one heart between the two of them, and it was the sister who had it all . . .

Volodya A. went missing in the South—that same summer of 1919.

Irina, who sang Galli-da, died in 1920 in a state children's home.[VII]

Evgeny Bagrationovich Vakhtangov died a long time ago in Russia.

Vakhtang Levanovich Mchedelov died a long time ago in Russia.

Yura S. (who gave Alya the sweet bun) died here in Paris, after becoming famous.

The other Yura—N. (with whom we climbed to the roof)—I don't know what happened to him.

Alya left for Moscow in 1937 to become an artist.

The house in Boris and Gleb Lane is still standing. Of my two poplars, one remains.

I said the characters. Essentially, there were no characters in my story. There was only love. It was love acting through people.

***

The more life I give to you, the more I die, I withdraw from life toward you, I die in you. The closer you get, the further I move away. It's as if the barrier between the living and the dead has already been lifted, and they come and go freely in time and space—and in their opposites. My death is the reward for your life. To awaken the shadows of Hades, it was necessary to nourish them with fresh blood. But I've gone further than Ulysses, I nourished you with mine.

***

29th of April, 1922, Russia—a heading like I'd write at that time, in the manner of the people. I'm going abroad in an hour. It is all over.

There was a knock on the door. On the threshold was Pavlik A., whom I hadn't seen for a year, perhaps.

Eyes wide with horror, even more enormous, solemn eyes. A voice in the same register (he had a powerful voice, strange for such a small body), but this time more powerful than possible: a veritable voice booming from Hades:

"I . . . found out . . . I mean Evgeny said that you . . . are . . . Are you going abroad today?"

"Yes, Pavlik."

"Marina Ivanovna, may I . . . ?"

"No. I only have an hour before I leave. I have to . . . collect my thoughts, say goodbye to places . . ."

"But—only one minute?"

"It's already passed, Pavlik."

"But let me tell you anyway, I have to tell you (a big gulp)—Marina, I deeply regret every minute of these years that I didn't spend with you . . ."

(My hair stood on end—the same words from Sonechka's letter . . . So now, from the lips of her poet, she was saying goodbye to me?!)

"Pavlik, there's no time left, there's only one thing: if you ever loved me, even just a little—find my Sonechka Gollidey for me."

He was so hurt his voice choked:

"I promise you."

***

Now—the em dash. A dash that's three thousand miles and seven years long: two thousand five hundred and fifty-five days.

I was walking with my two-year-old son in the park near the Bellevue Observatory. Next to me, on my other hand, in step with my two-year-old son, was Pavlik, who came here with the Vakhtangov Studio [to Paris]. He already had two daughters and (I believe?) a son.

"And . . . my Sonechka?"

"Gollidey is married and acting in the provinces."

"Is she happy?"

"I can't really say."

***

And that's all.

***

Another dash—even longer: ten whole years. 14th of May, 1937, Friday. We were getting off at the Mairie d'Issy metro station, Mur (the two-year-old, now twelve) and I. We were almost at the Provence boutique and he said to me (or rather to himself):

"American Sunday is their Dimanche Illustre!"

"What does Holiday mean?"

"A day off, or a vacation."

"Yes, it means—a celebration. It was the last name of the woman I loved more than any other woman in the world. Or maybe more than anything in the world. More than anyone—Sonechka Gollidey. Mur, if you could only have a wife like that!"

He said angrily: "Ma-a-ma!"

"I'm not saying she herself, she's not young anymore. She was three years younger than me."

"I don't want to marry an old woman! I don't want to get married at all."

"Silly. I'm not saying: Sonechka Gollidey, but someone like Sonechka. However—there aren't any like her, so you can calm down—and in general no one is worthy of her."

"Mother! I don't even know her, you're talking about something only you know—I mean, you can tell me . . ."

"But you're not interested . . ."

(He was already thinking about the newsstand waiting for him at the corner of Raspail Boulevard, with American Mickey Mouse comics:)

"I guess, it's interesting . . ."

"Mur, you know, she was like a little girl"—I said, searching for the right word—"and a real little demon! She had two long, long brown braids . . . (Mur made an involuntary grimace and said: like the time of hair and horses!) . . . and she was so small . . . much smaller than you (his grimace grew)—because you're already bigger than me . . . (teasing him) and so brave: she carried meals to the *cadets* under gunfire in the Cathedral of Christ the Savior . . ."

"Why were these *cadets* eating in the church?"

"Doesn't matter why. The important thing is it was under gunfire. When I said goodbye to her, I said: Sonechka, whatever happens to me, as long as you exist, everything will be fine. She was the most beautiful thing I had ever seen in my life, the sweetest thing I'd ever eaten in my life . . . (Mur: Ugh, Mama!) She wrote letters to me, and in the last one: Marina! How I love your hands that should only be kissed, but they have moved cabinets and lifted tons . . ."

"Well, that really is romantic! Why kissed?"

"Because . . . because . . . (taking the offensive)—and do you have something to say about it?"

"Nothing, but if, for example, she wrote (hesitating) . . . If they could only smell the scent of flowers . . ."

Then after understanding, confused, he laughed in embarrassment.

"Yes, that's right Mur, there are two nostrils on each finger! How many nostrils in all, Mur??"

(We both laughed. I went on:) "And she told me one more thing: Marina! To know that you exist is to know that there is no death."

"Well, of course, for you, that is flattering."

"What does that have to do with it?! She simply told the truth, the truth at the time, and she emanated such a force of emotion—me too, even now, for that matter—there is just as much . . . but no one wants it!"

"Yes, yes, of course, I understand, I know, but still . . ."

"I absolutely have to write to Alya. I want her to look for her. Because I have to let her know that in my entire life, I've never had anyone, I've never been so . . ."

We arrived at the metro and the conversation was over.

***

Small dash—just for one day:

15th of May, 1937, Saturday. A thick letter from Russia—by air. I open it and the first thing I saw, right at the end: Sonechka Gollidey—I already knew.

This is what I already knew: "Mama! I forgot to write to you! I found traces of Sonechka Gollidey, your Sonechka, but it was much too late. She died last year from liver cancer—but didn't suffer. She didn't know that she had cancer. She was one of the best performers in the provinces and only two years ago she came to Moscow. They say she was so incredibly talented . . ."

***

And here is the second piece of news, already known far and wide: the story of the sister of one of Sonechka's friends—written down by Alya and sent to me:

She married the director of the theater in the countryside. He loved her very much and was very devoted to her. Sonya spent all those years—1924 until her death—in the provinces, but she came to Moscow quite often. We all tried to persuade her to get work and settle in Moscow, but somehow she didn't know how to go about it. Of course, if Vakhtangov had stayed alive, her whole life would have gone differently. K. [an actor] loved her very much, in fact he was a gentle and kind person, but he didn't know how to help her at all. Besides, he had a very jealous family, and it was difficult for Sonechka to visit them . . . It was painful. She rarely saw Zavadsky. Very rarely. And Stanislavsky? For a while he was very much in love with her and her talent, but his infatuations did not last.

She should have only done readings, but she was so attached to the theater! She was distracted. But the theater, of course, it would be more difficult. In the countryside, with theater groups she was, well . . . a jewel, really! But she rarely got good roles. If she had recited—all alone on stage—can you imagine that? Yes, she was small. She often played children's roles. How she loved the theater! But if you knew how she acted—no, not only in the dramatic sense (I didn't see her act much, she worked mostly in the provinces)—but she was a real hero. Several years ago she began to have terrible stomach pains. And so she'd sit backstage with a hot water bottle then go on stage, act out the scene, and then, as soon as the curtain fell, she'd grab the hot water bottle again.

But why, when these pains began, didn't she go see a doctor, why wasn't she taken to a doctor?"

When she came to Moscow, she went to a very good homeopath. He gave her medicine, and the pain went away. After that, she only went to this homeopath. She lived like this for four years and felt good. The last time she came to Moscow, I saw that she had lost a lot of weight, all she had left was her huge eyes devouring her face. She had changed a lot, but she didn't know it, and even when she looked in the mirror, she didn't see it. Then her husband told me there was nothing she could do.

We called the doctor, and he said he would call a surgeon. The surgeon examined her carefully and asked if she had a family history of cancer. She said no. Then he said that she needed to go to the hospital. Obviously, we kept what she had a secret from her. She really didn't want to go to the hospital, and she cried all the time and said: This is going to end in a coffin! This is the coffin! But in the hospital she calmed down and became composed and began to make all sorts of plans. She had surgery. The surgeon saw that it was too late. Doctors said she had only a few days to live.

Her husband and my sister came to see her all the time. She didn't know she was dying. She talked constantly about how she would live and work in the future. On the day she died her sister was there, and her husband too, and there was someone else. Sofia Evgenievna loved order. She asked my sister to tidy everything up in the room (she had a room by herself). They brought her a lot of flowers, and my sister put them in a vase and tidied everything. Sonya said: Now I'll go to sleep. She turned over, settled into bed and fell asleep. And she died in her sleep.

I don't know the hour or date of her death. I was not in Moscow. My sister probably knows. It was probably in the evening. When was it? In the summer, yes, that's right, in the summer. The Chelyuskins arrived then by plane.

She talked about your mother [Marina] very, very often. She often told us about her and about you, and often she read your mother's poems to us. No, she never ever forgot.

. . . After Sonya's death, her husband went somewhere and disappeared. Where he is now—is unknown.

Sonya was cremated.

When the Chelyuskin sailors flew in . . . it was the summer of 1934. This meant not one year ago but three whole years ago. But whether a year—three—or three days—I would never see her again, which I always knew would happen, and she would never know how . . .

No! she always knew—and forever!

"When the Chelyuskins flew in"—it sounds like: "When the swallows flew in" . . . a natural phenomenon, and wasn't that better, its freedom, and simplicity, and the simplicity of the people—this vague mention of the exact hour and dates?

After all, our beginning with her was never on a particular date, but at the time of the first little green leaves . . .

Yes, it burned me up that Sonechka was cremated, burned, that there was no cross—to inscribe—as she had requested:

. . . Everything ended with the refrain:

My dearest little one!

Actually I see her in the fire, I don't see her in the ground! She did not at all have that submission and patience that was equally required for a body or a seed that had not germinated. There was nothing like a seed, she was all this:

I know my origins!
I am a flame, insatiable,
I consume and am consumed.
The embers when I embrace,
Ashes when I pass by
I am truly a flame!

It incensed me, too, not knowing where to go—if that happens one day—there would be nowhere to go and nowhere above to stay and reflect. The idea that Sonechka no longer exists at all, not even her little bones. Sonechka and her bones . . . no!

Infanta, know this, what does the pyre matter . . .

The first thing I heard about her was: the pyre, the last: they burned her. The first thing I heard about her was: fire and the last too: fire.

How strange that these lines from Pavlik came true but in reverse:

I will go up there, I am ready—if I can be sure
That your eyes will be there contemplating me

After all, it was the Infanta who was being burned and the Dwarf watched. He—the wise Dwarf, chastened with white hair—watched Infanta, eternally young, burning but not consumed!

If I could have my way—I would have taken her ashes and scattered them from the top of the highest mountain (still destined for me to climb) to the four corners of the earth—toward all those beloved: those who haven't yet been loved and those who are yet to be loved. Even if it could be from the top of Sparrow Hills (which we never got to climb together: I had children and queues at the stores to stand in . . . and her—love . . .)

But what if we were doing just that? Doing just that—neither from any mountain, nor from a hill: I'd scatter the ashes from the flat palm of an ocean moor—for your love for all, the you who have been and the you who will be?

***

. . . And now—farewell, Sonechka!

May you be blessed for the moments of bliss and happiness you gave to another heart, lonely and grateful!

My God! A full minute of bliss! Isn't it enough for a lifetime?

***

(Lacanau-Ocean, Summer, 1937)

The Girlfriend Poems —The Traditional Cycle I

1

Are you really happy?—I can't tell!
Are you better off—not saying?
Methinks you've kissed so many.
That's why—the melancholy.

All of Shakespeare's tragic heroines
I see in you.
The tragic genteel lady,
No one could save!

You must be tired of repeating love
Recitatives.
Metallic bracelet on pale hand—
Eloquence.

"I love you!"—Like a storm cloud
Hovering—sinful, I know!
For you are sarcastic and fiery,
And better than anyone else,

For us, our lives, we, are—so different
On the dark roads of life,
For your inspiring seductions
And your obscure fate.

For, you know, I'll say I'm sorry,
My demonic one with a high forehead,
For—whatever happens—hell!
There's no way to save you.

Or this my trembling—can I
Can I be dreaming?—
For this strange delight
That you are not a *he.*

October 16, 1914

2

Cuddling under my plush comforter,
I send for yesterday's dreams.
What was that?—Who won?
Who was conquered?

I revisit all those dreams
Suffering through them once more.
I just can't find the words
Was it indeed love?

Who was the hunter? Who the prey?
Everything turned around to hell.
What did the wise Siberian cat know
With that long purr of his?

In that contest of wills,
Whose hands caught the ball?
Whose heart: yours or mine—
Pounded at a gallop?

And anyway—what was all that?
What is it we want so much,
Yet regret? I don't even know:
Did I win? Was I conquered?

October 23, 1914

3

Today, it was thawing. At the window
I waited out the melting snow
My mind sober—my bosom relaxed,
I'm peaceful once more.

I don't know why, perhaps, my soul
Simply got tired and worn out
Somehow my rebellious pencil
Did not want to move.

I waited it out—in the fog—
Far away from good and evil,
Quietly drumming my finger
On the barely ringing glass.

My soul is not better or worse
Than any passing stranger,
Than this pearly puddle of water
Where the heavens have splashed,

Than a bird flying by
Or simply, a dog running.
Even she, the destitute singer,
Could not bring me to tears.

The sweet outmoded art
The soul has learned so well.
Some great feeling was
Thawing in my soul today.

October 24, 1914

4

You didn't feel like getting dressed
You didn't feel like getting up from your chair.
—But every one of your days to come
Would be happier with my happiness!

You worried so much about going out
Late at night, in the dark and the cold.
—But every one of your hours to come
Would be carefree with my happiness!

You didn't really mean any harm
Innocent and irreparable.
—I became your youth,
And it's passing us by!

October 25, 1914

5

Today at eight o'clock at breakneck speed
On the Bolshaya Lubyanka[II],
Like a shot, a snowball, whizzed past,
A sleigh to some mysterious spot.

Laughter echoed in the distance . . .
I watched frozen in disbelief:
That reddish, fur-like hair
Someone tall—stood beside you!

You were with another woman
With her, you cleared the sleigh path,
She, the one you desire and held close—
More so than me—your beloved!

The world was merry and the evening easy!
Your packages flew out of your muff . . .
You rushed about in the snowy whirlwind,
Eye to eye, shoulder to shoulder.

It was such a raging storm
And snow fell, so white, so white.
All in the space of two seconds—
—Not more—as I looked after you!

I stroked the firm fluff
Of my fur coat—with no anger.
Your little Kai has frozen
Oh my Snow Queen, my queen!

October 26, 1914

6

How gaily your gray fur coat glistened
With freshly fallen flakes, and my sable one.
How we combed the Christmas market
For ribbons brighter than all the rest.

How greedily I filled up on waffles
Rosy and savory—all six!
How in your honor,[III] I was touched
By all the little chestnut horses!

How the men in chestnut waistcoats
Puffed up like sails, peddling their rags.
How the foolish countrywomen marveled
At the strange Moscow ladies.

How at the time the crowd dispersed,
We chanced to step into the cathedral.
How you fixed your gaze upon
The old icon of Mother Mary!

How her countenance with its downcast
Eyes looked pious and weary
In the icon case, surrounded
By plump Elizabethan cupids.

How you abandoned my arm
And cried, "Oh, I want her!"
And painstakingly placed
In the holder—a glowing candle . . .

—Such a worldly hand, adorned
With an opal ring! I was so overcome!—
How I promised to steal
The icon for you that night.

How in the convent guesthouse—
With bells clanging and sun setting
Blissful as birthday girls, we let loose
Like a regiment of soldiers.

How I vowed to grow more beautiful
With age for you and spilled salt,
How three times I threw the king of hearts—
And you were in such a rage!—

How you grabbed my head
Caressing every curl,
How the little flower on your
Enamel broach cooled my lips.

How I brushed my sleepy cheek
Against your slender fingers,
How you teased me like a boy,
How you liked me that way . . .

December 1914

7

That night, over coffee grounds,
She sobbed, gazing eastward.
Mouth innocent and licentious
Like a monstrous flower.

Soon the moon, slender and new,
Will replace the scarlet sun.
How many more combs and bangles
Will I give you as presents!

The young moon will not watch
Over anyone between branches.
How many more trinkets can I gift you—
Bracelets, earrings, necklaces!

Beneath your heavy mane of hair
Let those pupil halos peer out!
Are they your jealous companions?
Thoroughbred horses are easy.

December 5, 1914

8

Her neck rises freely
Like a wild shoot.
What's her name, her age,
Where's she from? What's her story?

The curve of her pale lips—
Whimsical and wanton,
But dazzling is her
Beethoven's brow.

A light brown encircles
Her eyes, lightly shaded,
Eyes like two moons
Hold sway over her face.

Her melancholy visage
Moves me to distraction.
Hand that goes well with a whip
Decked with an opal—set in silver.

Such a hand, swathed in silk,
Suitable for a violin bow,
Incomparable hand,
Such a beautiful hand.

January 10, 1915

9

I refrain from touching your hand,
You are on your own path,
Yet the anguish inside me feels endless,
I wish you were not so special to me.

My heart instantly cried out, "Darling!"
As I forgave you everything—on a whim
Not knowing a thing about you—even your name!
I said: Oh love me, please love me!

I can see the curl of your lips—
Their arrogance, accentuated
By your brow's heavy ledge:
This heart has been taken by storm!

Your dress—a black silk coat of armor,
Your voice with its hint of gypsy huskiness,
I love everything about you till it hurts—
Yes, even that you are not a beauty!

But beauty won't fade over time!
You're not a flower but a stalk of steel,
Nastier than nasty, sharper than sharp—
Kidnapped—from what island?

You clown around—with that fan and cane,
But in every fiber of your being, every bone,

In every one of your long nasty fingers—
Is the tenderness of a woman, the brashness of a boy.

Fending off those snickers with poetry,
I reveal myself for you and the world—
So much is ahead of us because of you,
Mystery woman with the look of Beethoven!

January 14, 1915

10

How can I ever forget that scent
Of White Rose perfume and tea,
The Sèvres porcelain figurines
On the mantel above a blazing fire . . .

I—in a luxurious dress
Fashioned in golden silk,
You in a knitted black jacket
With a fancy winged collar.

I remember how you looked when
You entered, not the slightest blush,
How you stood there, your finger at your lips,
Slightly tilting your head.

Your commanding brow, under the weight
Of your reddish helmet of hair—
Not a woman and not a boy
But something stronger than me!

With a futile flourish I rose,
And all of them surrounded us.
With a laugh, someone blurted:
"Gentlemen, get acquainted!"

Stretching out your hand
You sweetly placed it on mine,
And like a sliver of ice it
Lingered lightly in my palm.

Already foreseeing a clash
With one man glaring sideways,
I half-reclined in the armchair,
Twirling the ring on my finger.

You pulled out a cigarette,
I offered you a light,
Not knowing what I'd do if you
Looked me straight in the eye.

I remember—how our wineglasses
Clinked over the blue vase.
"Oh, be my Orestes!"[IV]
As I presented you with a flower.

Are you amused—by my remark?
Pulling out a handkerchief from
Your suede bag with a long gesture
You let it slip from your hand.

January 28, 1915

11

Everyone's eyes sting under the sun—
Not one day is like the other.
I tell you this in case
I were to betray you.

Whose lips I happen to kiss
In a moment of love and affection,
To whomever I may make a promise
Ominous at the midnight hour—

Thrive, says a mother to her child,
Bloom like a flower in the sun.
Never stray in any one direction,
Never choose one over another.

Do you see the little cypress cross?
—Oh you know it so well!—
Just whistle beneath my window
And all will be aroused again!

February 22, 1915

12

I'll say it again on this eve of parting,
On the day before love's end,
That I've truly loved your
Commanding, powerful hands.

And your eyes—they don't bestow
Their gaze on just anyone!—
Yet they demand an accounting
For any casual glance of mine.

God sees all of this!—you,
Your damned possessiveness
Demanding retribution
For my accidental sighs!

Once more I'll say, I'm tired of it.
—Don't take this the wrong way!—
It was your soul that crossed
And hindered mine.

Once more I'll say: Listen!—
It doesn't matter! It's over!—
My mouth before your first kiss
Was much too young and innocent.

My look—before your first look—
Bold and brilliant. And my heart—
Like a five-year-old's . . . Happy the soul
Who never met up with you on earth!

April 28, 1915

13

There are names like sultry flowers
And gazes like dancing flames . . .
Certain lips are dark and sinuous,
With deep and moist corners.

Some women—have hair like helmets,
Their fans flutter ominously but delicately.
They're thirty years old. What do you need?
From me and my Spartan boy's soul?![V]

The Ascension, 1915

14

I ask the murky mirror
Where my dreams seem turbid and misty—
I ask where your path will lead you
And where you'll take refuge.

I see the boat's tall mast
And you—standing on the deck . . .
You shrouded—in the steam of the train . . .
Fields in evening mourning . . .

Dew drops on evening fields,
Crows hover—over them . . .
I bless you to the four
Corners of the earth!

May 3, 1915

15

If the first one you loved—
Was the height of beauty,
Curls with hints of henna,
Plaintive call of the *zurna*,
The ring of flint—beneath horse hooves,
And her graceful leap down.
And her two ornate slippers—
Embroidered in flowers.

The second—the one you loved next—
Her thinly arched eyebrows,
Silken carpets
From pink-roofed Bukhara,
Hands full of rings,
A mole on her cheek,
Eternal sun on her blonde hair,
And London at midnight.

The third one for you
Was somewhat sweeter . . .
—What part of me will endure
In your heart, you wanderer?

July 14, 1915

Restored Poems by Tsvetaeva to Parnok[1]

Blue-green hills of Moscow
Air slightly warm—tar and dust
I sleep all day, and laugh—I must
Be recovering from the dark winter.

I walk along as quietly as I can
Not regretting my unwritten poems!
Clatter of wheels, scent of roasted almonds
More precious than any quatrain.

My head is delightfully empty
Only because my heart—is too full!
My days are like little waves
On which I gaze from the bridge.

Someone's glances seem way too tender
And in this gentle not quite warm air
I already feel sick with the summer
After just recovering from winter.

March 13, 1915

Just remember this: dearer to me than
Anyone else is one strand of my own hair.
So go on your way . . . You too.
And you also, and you, and you.

Go on—fall out of love with me, all of you!
Don't watch over me in the mornings
Let me peacefully go out and
Stand in the wind.

May 6, 1915

In days gone by you were like a mother to me
I could call on you during the night,
A delirious light, a restless light,
The light of my life in days gone by.

Benevolent one, do you remember
The sun never set on those days gone by,
They were motherly and daughterly,
Sunset-less, twilight-less.

Farewell, I did not come to trouble you,
I just wish to kiss the hem of your gown,
And behold you eye to eye—eyes
Rained with kisses in days gone by.

The day will come—I'll die—and you will too,
The day will come—I'll understand—and you will . . .
And we'll return to the day of forgiveness
To those irretrievable days gone by.

April 26, 1916

Clocks chime—what time is it?
They've been ringing.
The depth of those huge eyes,
Flowing satin dresses . . .
I can barely make you out,
Barely see you.

The neighbor's porch light
Has gone out
Somewhere lovers make love
Endlessly. The outline
Of your face is scary.

In the room's half-light
Night—harmonious
Pierced with moonlight
The window's recess—
Is like an ice floe.

"Did you give up?"—I was asked
"I never tried."
A voice—moonstruck.
A voice—a hundred miles away
That voice!

A moonbeam came between us,
That moved the world.
Dark red metal hair
That crazy hair
Shining relentlessly.

The course of history forgotten
In the bright moon's course.

Mirror splits the moon in two
The distant ring of hooves
The creak of a wagon.

The street lamp has gone out
The bright path dims
Soon the rooster will crow
All for the separation
Of two young women.

November 1, 1914

Voices and their play of promises
Glances furious and dark,
Mouths fiery, smoldering,
And those fatal lips—

Oh, I fought too easily with you!
So—what are you doing with me now,
Why mock me with that familiar
Chill—in your voice, your eyes.

March 14, 1915

In the bluish, fog of incense
With panels like silver—
An unexpected feather
Flies up towards us.

Our glances cross
Trembling—we pray—for what?
Your voice's melody is
Like Bohemian crystal.

Moment of longing and desire,
Movement—a long moan,
Your bright face immersed
In the waves of gray fog.

It lasted only a moment
Setting sail . . . floating away
My rival!—I expected
To be no less beautiful!

September 5, 1915

A gypsy-like passionate breakup!
You ran away—as soon as you saw me.
Dropping my head into my hands,
I think, looking into the night:

No one rummaging through our letters
Would realize the depth
Of our betrayals, I mean—
How true we were to ourselves.

October 1915

The full moon, my fur coat
The lightest dance of bells . . .
What a carefree time!—But for me
It was so profound, that time,

The headwind gave me wisdom,
The snow softened my gaze.
On the hill, the monastery
Gleamed with snow—and holiness.

You kissed away the snowflakes
From my fur coat, dear friend.
I looked at the tree—in the field
And then at the lunar circle.

Behind the coachman's back
Our two heads have not yet met
The Lord began—to appear to me
And you have fallen asleep.

November 27, 1915

Letter to an Amazon[I]

I've read your book. You are dear to me like all women writers. Don't be offended by this "all"—all of them do not write: only certain women write.

So, you are close to me like any unique being and, especially, like any unique woman.

I think of you ever since the day I first saw you—was it only a month ago? When I was young, I longed to say: I'm afraid of the wave rising within me and taking me to another [...] I'm afraid of not being able to love again, not knowing how to recognize it again. But I am no longer young, and I've learned to let go of almost everything—forever.

To have so much to say and not open my lips. To have so much to give—and not unclench my hand. This detachment you call a bourgeois virtue and, bourgeois or not, virtue or not, it is the main source of my actions. The source? Denial? Yes, for the suppression of force requires an infinite effort greater than its free expression—which does not require any effort at all. In this sense, every natural activity is passive, and all conscious passivity is active (effusion-effortless, repression-action). What is more difficult: to keep a horse from running or to let it run, and, since the horse we hold back is us—of these two which is more painful: to be held back or to set our energy free? To breathe or not to breathe? Do you remember the children's game in which the person who wins is the one who can stay the longest in a suffocating chest? A cruel game and not very bourgeois.

To act or let go? Every time I deny myself I feel an earthquake inside of me. It is I, the earth, that quakes. Denial. A struggle petrified.

My denial is also this: do not condescend—do not question the existing order of things. And in our case, what is the existing order of things? To read your book, to thank you in words empty of myself, to see you from time to time "smiling in such a way that they don't see you smiling"—behave as if you have never written anything and I have never read anything: as if nothing had ever been.

I could have done that, I can still do that, but for once I don't want to.

Listen to me, you do not have to answer, just listen. This is a wound straight to the heart, to the heart of your cause, of your belief, of your body, of your heart.

There is one big gap in your book, only one, but an enormous one—was it conscious or not? I don't believe in the unconsciousness of thinking beings, even less so in the unconsciousness of women writers, especially.

This big blank gap, this black hole—is the Child.

You return to it constantly, you give him in frequency what you owe it in importance, you plant him here and there, and there again, depriving him of the one shout you owe him.

This shout—is it possible you've never even heard it? "If only I could have a baby with you!"

This jealousy, fierce and unique in the world, implacable because it is incurable, incomparable to anything usual, anyone "normal," incomparable even to maternal jealousy. This jealousy is a premonition of the inevitable break, those wide-open eyes fixed on a baby she would one day want and that you the beloved cannot give her. Those eyes riveted on the child to come.

"Lovers do not have children." Yes, but they die. All of them. Romeo and Juliet, Tristan and Iseult, the Amazon [Queen Penthesilea] and Achilles, Siegfried and Brunhilda (these all-powerful lovers, together-apart, whose loving separation prevails over their complete union . . .) And there are others . . . and more . . .

of all songs, of all times, all places . . . They have no time for the future, which is the child; they have no child because there is no future, they have only the present, which is their love, always in the present. They die—or it's their love that dies (degenerates into friendship, into motherhood: old Baucis and her old Philemon, old Pulcheria and her old child, Athanasius—couples as monstrous as they are touching).

Love in itself is childhood. Lovers are children. Children don't have children.

Or—like Daphnis and Chloe—we don't know much about them: even if they survived—they died in us, for us.

One cannot live on love alone. The only thing that survives love is the Child.

And that other shout, haven't you heard that either?—"How I'd love to have a child myself—without a man!" The smiling sigh of a young girl, the hopeless sigh of an old maid, and sometimes the desperate sigh of a woman—"How I would love one—only my *own*!"

And here the smiling young girl who does not want a stranger in her body, who wants neither him nor anything from him, who only wants what is mine, meeting at the crossroads another me, a *she*, who she doesn't have to fear, from whom she does not have to defend herself, for the other one cannot do her any harm, just as one (at least being young) cannot do harm to oneself. A certainty that is very illusory and wavers from the first glimmer of the girlfriend's distrust only to be crushed by the heavy blows that come from the surge of her hatred.

But let's not anticipate: for the moment she is still happy and carefree, free to love from her heart, without a body, to love without fear, to love without doing any harm.

And when harm is done—she discovers this is not harm at all. The harm—is [...] shame, regret, remorse, disgust. Harm is the betrayal of her soul by a man, the betrayal of her childhood by the enemy. But there is no enemy because it is still me, always me, a new me yet one who has been asleep inside of me and awakened by this other me—there, before me, externalized at last, and finally *lovable.* She did not need to deny herself in order to become a woman; she only needed to let herself go (to the very depths of her being)—and let herself be. No crack, no break, no stigma.

And these words sum it up: "Oh me! Oh dearest me!"

Oh! It is never out of shame or disgust that she leaves her. It is because of and for something entirely different.

In the beginning it is almost a joke. "What a beautiful little baby!" "Wouldn't you like one too?" "Yes." "Nothing." "One like you—yes." "But . . . Well, that's laughable."

Another time a sigh. "How I would like . . ." "What?" "Nothing." "Yes, yes, I know." "Because you know it—that is—but one *with you . . .*" Silence.

"You're still thinking about that?" "You said . . . I mean, you yourself said it."

She herself doesn't need anything, but she must give much too much, all that is left of herself to her. "I would have liked to have loved you as a little girl"—just as a woman would say: I would have liked to have loved you as a little boy. Again you. Again a little you. A you, born of me.

Finally, it becomes a shout of desperation— stark, irrevocable. "A child with you!"

The one who will never come. The one whose coming one cannot even pray for. One can ask the Virgin for a child from a lover, one can ask the Virgin for a child from an old man—the first a sin—the second a miracle—but one cannot ask for madness. A union which absolutely excludes a child. A state of things implying the absence of a child. Unthinkable. Everything but a child. Just as at a king's or gentleman's dinner, everything is there but bread. The great daily feminine bread.

It is never simply the urgent desire of the one, the younger woman, the one who is more she. The older one does not need a child, she has her girlfriend for her motherhood. "You are my girlfriend, you are my god, you are my everything."

But the other doesn't want to be loved like a child, she wants a child to love.

And the one who began with not wanting a child from him will end up wanting a child from her. And it is because this cannot be that she will leave her one day, still loving but harassed by the obvious and helpless jealousy of the other—and that again one day she will fall, shipwrecked, into the arms of the first person who comes along.

(My baby, my woman lover, my all, and, Madame, your ingenious word,—my female brother, never sister. One could say that the word sister evokes a certain fear in them, as if it might forcefully reinstate them in the world they have left forever.)

To begin with, the older woman fears the child more than the other desires it. One could say that the older one instills in her friend despair, transforms the smile into a sigh, the sigh into wish, the wish into obsession. It is the older woman's obsession that creates the younger woman's obsession. "You'll leave, you'll leave, you'll leave. You want the baby from me, you will want it from the first man who comes along . . . You are thinking about it again . . . You looked at that man. What a good father he would make for your child—right? Go then, since I can't give that to you.

Our apprehensions evoke, our fears suggest, our obsessions incarnate. Forced to be silent about this, the young woman thinks about it constantly, she only has eyes for young women with their arms full. And the thought that I will never have one, for never, never will I leave her. (That is the very moment that she leaves.)

The child—a fixed point from which she will henceforth not remove her eyes. The child repressed rises to the surface of her eyes like a drowning person. One must be blind not to see him there.

And the one who in the beginning wanted a child by her will ends up wanting a child from anyone: from the very him [...] abhorred. The persecutor becomes the rescuer. The Friend—the Enemy. And the wind returns to its circling.

The child begins within us long before its own beginning. There are pregnancies that last for years of hope, for eternities of despair.

And all the women friends who marry. And all the husbands of these friends, so fun-loving, so open, so close . . . And to think that I could also . . .

Be immured.

Be buried alive.

And the other one gets worked up. Allusions, suspicions, reproaches. The young woman: "Don't you love me anymore?" "I love you but—you will leave me."

You'll leave, you'll leave, you'll leave.

Before leaving she will want to die. Then, in the throes of death, without knowing anything, without premeditating anything, without thinking anything, by the pure and triple instinct for life—youth, time, insides—she will agree to a rendezvous, never missed, needing to laugh and joke on the other side of town—and of life—with whomever—the husband of one of her friends or a subordinate of her father, as long as it is not her.

The man, after the woman, what simplicity, what kindness, what frankness. What liberty! What purity.

Then it will be the end. The beginning of the lover? The lovers' journey? The stability of a husband?

It will be the Child.

I omit the exceptional case: the woman without a maternal instinct.

I omit also the common case: the corrupted lady, whether by nature or by fashion: the generally insignificant creature of pleasure.

I omit also the rare case of the tormented soul, the person who, in love, searches for the soul, therefore—predestined for a woman.

And the great lover, the woman who, in love, searches for love and takes the good wherever she finds it.

And the clinical case.

I take the normal case, the natural and vibrant case of the young female being who fears men and goes toward women and wants to have a baby. The being who—given a stranger, someone indifferent, even the enemy-liberator and the oppressive woman lover—in the end chooses the enemy.

The one who wants to have a child more than to be in love.

The one who loves her child more than her love.

For the Child is an innate possession, it exists in us before love, before the lover. Their desire to be is what makes us open our arms. A young girl, I'm speaking about those from the North, is always too young for love, but never too young for a child. At thirteen she dreams of one.

An innate possession that must be given to us. Some begin by loving the donor, others finish by loving him, and still others end up submitting to him, and then others by no longer submitting to him.

An innate possession that must be given to us. He who does not give this to us takes it from us.

And we will find her again, arms full and hearts full of hatred toward the woman she will henceforth call ungrateful like all those who no longer love, unjust like all who still love—a youthful mistake.

She cannot.

Do not be upset with me. I am responding to the Amazon, not to the pale white feminine vision that wants nothing from me. Not to the one who gave me the book but to the one who wrote it.

If you had never mentioned the child, I would have seen this as a conscious omission, a complete renunciation by silence, a scar that I would have respected. But you always come back to the same thing, you throw it back like a ball: "What right do they have to create or destroy life? Two children—two neglected ones," etc.

This is the only weak point, the only vulnerable point, the only breach in this perfect entity which is two women who love each other. The impossible thing is not to resist the temptation of a man but to resist the need for a child.

The only weak point that undermines all of this. The only vulnerable point through which the enemy army can enter. For even if one day we would be able to have a child without him, we will never be able to have a child with her, a little "you" to love.

And even if the miracle came true, open your eyes and what would you have: two mothers.

(An adopted daughter? Neither yours nor mine? With two mothers, on top of it all? Let nature have its way.)

The child, the only vulnerable point that ruins the cause. The only saving grace for men. And for humanity.

An entity too complete. A unity, too one. ("Two will make one." No . . . two will make three.) A road that leads to nowhere. A dead end. Let's retrace our steps.

You may be beautiful, you may be the Only One—the first zero will triumph over you. A zero that will be blessed. Meanwhile you will remain cursed.

But this is the same case as not being able to have a child with a certain man. Is that any reason to leave him?

An exceptional case cannot be compared to a law that has no exception. It is the entire tribe, the entire relationship, the entire thing that is condemned in every case of love between women.

To leave the sterile man for his fertile brother is something other than leaving the eternally sterile woman for an eternally fertile male enemy. In one, I say farewell to only one man, in the other, I say farewell to the entire species, the entire cause, to all women in one.

Replace only the object [...]. Change the riverbanks—and the world.

Oh! I know sometimes this goes on until death. A touching and terrifying scene [...] on a wild Crimean shore, of two middle-aged women who have lived their lives together. One of them is the sister of a great Slavic philosopher, who is now being read in France. The same luminous brow, the same stormy eyes, the same full, naked mouth. But they had around them a void more empty than around an old infertile "normal" couple, a void more isolating, more emptying.

Nothing, nothing but that—an accursed species.

Then again it could be that if the young woman is a deep person, it's the horror of this curse that makes her leave.

"What will society say of them"—does not mean anything, should not mean anything, since all that is said is badly said, everything it sees—badly seen. The evil eye of envy, of curiosity, of indifference. Society has nothing to say, it wallows in evil itself.

God? Once and for all, God does not have anything to do with carnal love. His name, joined or set in opposition to the name of a beloved, whether male or female, sounds like a sacrilege. There are some things that are incommensurable: Christ and carnal love. God has nothing to do with these trifles, except to heal us. He said once and for all—Love Me, forever. Everything else—is vanity. Absolute, incurable vanity. The very fact that I love a human being in this way betrays Him who, for my sake and that of others, died on the cross for another kind of love.

The Church and the State? They will have nothing to say about it as long as they pressure and bless thousands of young men to kill one another.

But what will Nature say about it, what, the only avenger and the only judge of our physical deviations. Nature says: no. By forbidding us this, she defends herself. God, by forbidding us one thing, does so out of love for us, while Nature, in forbidding us this, does so out of self-love, out of hatred toward everything that is not she. Nature hates the monastery as much as she hates the Island [Lesbos] on which the head of Orpheus[II] lands. Her vengeance is our downfall. It is only that in the monastery we have God to help us, while on the Island, only the sea in which to drown.

The Island—part of the land which is not, a land one cannot leave, a land one must love because one is condemned to it. A place from which everything can be seen, but from which nothing can be done.

A land with measured steps. A dead end.

The great dejected woman who was a great poetess chose the place of her birth well.[III]

A league of lepers.

Outside of nature. But how can a young girl, this being of nature, stray from the path, so completely, so confidently?

This is a spiritual trap. When she falls into the arms of her older woman, she falls neither into nature's trap nor that of the lover, who is too often seen as a seductress, a huntress, a raptor, even a vampire, while she is almost always, a noble and hurt being, whose only crime is that she "sees it coming" and—saying so in advance—sees the parting. The young woman falls into a spiritual trap.

She wants to love—but . . . she would love only—if . . . and when she is in the arms of the other woman, her head laying against the breast where the soul resides.

Push her away? Ask it of the old and young men.

. . . Then, comes the encounter. Unexpected and inevitable for—from this moment they live in two different worlds—the earth remains ever the same: the one they walk upon.

The heart leaps, an ebb and flow of blood. And the first and final weapon of a woman—the one that she disarms, believing she can even disarm death—her final pathetic semblance of courage—a live blade already red—her smile. Then there is a small incoherent torrent of syllables, running one after the other like ripples of water over pebbles. What did she say? Nothing, since the other woman did not hear anything, just as we never hear the first words, [...]. But the other woman's eyes, having left the animated mouth, perceives that this motion has a meaning: . . . ten months . . . a love . . . he likes me better than the rest . . . he presses . . . (Swallow this, take this in, take this in once more, take in every bit of it—for everything you have done to me [...]!) . . . I was saying—he presses . . . (More than the entire earth, more than the entire sea—on the heart of the Older Woman).

What voluptuous vengeance! And in her eyes—such hatred. The hatred of a servant finally freed. The pleasure she feels treading on that heart.

Finally this little flow is completely dammed up—only the undulations remain—slow, melodious, crystalline: "Wouldn't you like to see me, to see us, my husband and me . . ."

She didn't forget a thing. She remembers it all too much.

Then bathing the baby: a daily ritual, sacred.

The visible triumph—almost cynical—of his manhood. For, right away she has a son, always a son, as if Nature, hasty to claim her rights, didn't want to waste time on a girl. Not a little "you," imploring and impossible—but a little he, who comes by himself, comes by himself, not by request but on command, a simple result (a grand goal!)

The other woman clings to her last hope, or simply does not know what to say:

"He looks like you." "No." (drily and firmly) Gives him a dry and definite name. The final dart releasing perhaps the final residue of the powerful poison called love:

"He looks like his father. The spitting image of my husband." There is a deliberate vulgarity in this vengeful statement, choosing words that are the most hurtful, the most vulgar, the most everything (look at the normal person you loved!) By choice or by instinct? This happens naturally, she hears her own words (like once long ago she heard her own laughter . . .) Then after the ritual bath, when Moses is saved and wrapped in swaddling clothes, she gives him her breast and—then the supreme vengeance—feeding him, she watches the lowered eyes of the older one that flicker in envy, hidden in a mist of tenderness. For in the depths of every woman, if she isn't a monster, even in the heart of every monster . . . but there are no monsters among women.

She knows them well—this flicker, this smile—but for some reason, she does not lift her eyes.

If the man is sensitive, he will never ask her: "What are you thinking?"

Perhaps, when the older woman leaves, she'll want to beat her head against the wall.

Perhaps, when the other woman leaves, she'll not want affection.

If the man is sensitive, he will not embrace her immediately but wait—to embrace her—until after the other one has left—completely.

(Why did she come? To get hurt. Sometimes this is all that is left to us.)

Then there will be the other meeting, the counter-meeting, a retribution.

The very same earth (except for this, nothing else is worth mentioning, for everything that goes on, goes on within).

The same for spectators and audience. (Nature's final vengeance: the fact that they were too isolated, too together, too united, too one-for-the-other, that henceforth they will only see each other in the presence of others and everything will come between them.)

At the same time: Youth is eternal, as long as she exists.

"Look, isn't that your friend passing by?" "Where?" "That one, with the dark girl in blue."

Before seeing, she knows.

And here the human wave, more inhumane and inescapable, than the sea, brings her, leads her to . . .

This time the older woman begins: "How are you?" (and without waiting, without listening) "Allow me to introduce to you my friend, Miss so-and-so . . . (a name)." If the former one, whose blood has completely drained under her rouge, "was" blonde—the new one, the replacement will undoubtedly be a brunette. Charming—strong. Posthumous fidelity? Desire for complete death? Or a final blow to memories? Bitterness toward all blondes? Murder of a blonde by a brunette? It's the law. Ask men why.

There are looks that kill. That is not so in this case, the brunette goes away, very much alive, on the arm of the older woman lover. The flowing blue waves of her long dress physically separate her from the one who retreats with the never-ending seas.

At night, leaning over her sleeping lover: "Oh, John, if you only knew, if you only knew, if you only knew . . ."

It's not the day of the child's birth, it is today, three years later, when she has come to know what it has cost her.

As long as the other woman doesn't get old, she will always be seen accompanied by a living shadow.

The dark-haired woman will change: becoming light-haired again or red-haired. The dark-haired woman will leave her just like the fair one. Like all wanderers go on to their unknown goal—but always the same—resting for a moment under a tree which will never wander.

They will all—pass through. All would *pass through* there, if only . . . But one is not eternally young.

The older woman! Let's think about her. An island. Forever guarded. A mother, losing, one after the other, all her daughters, losing them forever, for they will not ask her to look after their children but, noticing her on the street corner, they will furtively make a sign of the cross on the child's blonde head. Niobe [queen of Thebes] with her feminine progeny, destroyed by that ferocious hunter. Forever losing at the only game that really matters—and that could be. Disgraced. Banished. Accursed. Pale, ghostlike vision, the tribe we do not identify except by a knowing look, of recognition, of appraisal [...] where the appraiser is joined with the idolater, and the chess player to the blessed—a look of many layers of various depth, where the last always turns out to be next-to-last, endless, bottomless, unaccountable, for it is an abyss—an indescribable look, effaced by the wintery smile of detachment.

Young women are recognized by their smiles, but older women's smiles are ignored.

Whether young or old, it is these women who have a spiritual appearance. All others have a physical appearance that do not belong to them, or do not belong to them yet.

She lives on an island. She creates an island. She herself is an island. An island with a vast colony of souls. Who knows, perhaps at this very moment, in the West Indies, there at the edge of the world . . . a young girl, tying back her dark hair in a bun . . .

The "Who knows" nourish.

And they are the only sure thing.

She will die alone for she is too proud to love a dog, and is too full of memories to adopt a baby. She wants neither animals, nor orphans, nor friends. She doesn't even want a young woman companion. King David, warming himself with the inanimate heat of Avizag, was a boor. She does not want paid warmth, an obligatory smile. She does not want to be a vampire or a grandmother. This may be good for a man who, in old age, is content with scraps, [...] the touch aimed for other shores, the touch of shoulders seeking other shoulders, and smiles moving to other lips—interrupted, accidentally stolen.

Go on, girls, go on . . . She will never be a poor relation at a celebration of someone else's youth. Neither with friendship nor respect nor the abyss of our own kindness, will she replace her love. She will never renounce that magnificent darkness, the round dark aureole burned far more magically than yours, Faust!—the fire of joy, long ago. She will stay firm—against all springtimes.

Even if a young woman were to throw herself at her like a child throws itself at a passerby or at a wall—she would retreat like the passerby but she would remain unshakeable like the wall. This fierce lover, when an old woman, will not lose her purity out of pride. She, who has inspired fear all her life, no longer wishes to intimidate. The young demon will never turn into an old hag.

Benevolence—condescension—distance.

Go on quickly, beautiful mad women . . .
Below the walls of the arsenal
Almost completely destroyed by time.
With a hand in front of your lamp—
Go on quickly, young girls, go on.

He goes by, however—surrounded by the legitimized glory of all the blondes of the past, while she—is surrounded by a mist of horror.

Neither God, nor other human beings, nor her self-pity can do anything about her and her natural inclinations, only her pride will be able to. And it alone will be able to. It would do so well that the eternally young girl, completely intimidated, would turn to her mother: "This lady frightens me. She has such a hard look. How have I displeased her?"

Almost destroyed by time—
Your hand before the radiance—
Go on, young women, go on . . .

And another girl, introduced to "this lady" by her mother—who knows why? —hears the lady speaking in a voice cracking with restraint: "Your mother told me that you have a predilection for painting. One must cultivate these talents, Mademoiselle . . ."

Never dolled up, never made up, never rejuvenated, never showing off or full of pretense, she leaves this to the aging "normal" women[IV], those who in the eyes of all, [. . .] with the blessings of a priest, in a lawful ceremony at age sixty marry a twenty-year old boy. She leaves all this to Caesar's sisters.

The natural and fatal inclination of the mountain toward the valley, of the river toward the lake, [...]

By evening the entire mountain surges back toward her summit, by evening it is the summit. One could say her rivers flow back the wrong way. By evening she recovers herself.

. . . Then, again, one day, the one who was once young will learn that somewhere at the other end of this very earth the older one has died. At first she will want to write in order to know. But time hurries on—the letter is frozen in time. Desire will remain desire. The "I want to know" becomes "I would like to know" then "I don't want to know anymore." And so what, if she has died? After all I, too, will die someday . . . With courage and with the highest honesty and indifference I say—

Hasn't she has died within me, and for me—already twenty years ago?

There's no need to die to be dead.

Island. Summit. Solitude.

Weeping willow! Inconsolable willow! Willow—body and soul of women! The willow's inconsolable neck. Gray hair swept back over her face, so she cannot see anything. Gray hair sweeping the face of the earth.

Water, air, mountains, trees are given to us in order to understand the human spirit, so deeply hidden away. When I see how a willow despairs, I understand—Sappho.

Clamart, November-December 1932.

(Copied and revised in November 1934, with a little more gray hair. M. T.)

Letter to Salomea Halpern[I]

Clamart (Seine) 101, Rue Condorcet, August 12, 1932

Dear Salomea,

You were in my dream last night. I felt such love and longing, such a mad love and longing, that my first thought, waking up, was—where have I been all these years, if I could have loved her so (if, clearly, I loved her so). And my first feeling upon waking up, was to tell you this—both about the dream last night (it was early morning) and my first thought this morning.

There were many others with you there. You were ill, but on your feet and quite beautiful (to distraction, endearingly so). It was twilight, everything was slightly dimmed, so that my longing (for love is a longing) my longing could be seen blazing. I kept asking when could I come to you—without everyone else around—I wanted to fall into you, like from a mountain into the abyss, and what happens to the soul there—I have no idea, but I know that it craves this, because the body must save itself. You were taking a stroll, a promenade—a kind of ritual—you were surrounded (but we were separated) by women friends (a kind of Greek chorus)—confidantes, whose faces I don't remember, and didn't even see. They were your background, the chorus—but it bothered me. Very close, at your feet, there was a dog—that gray one who died.

I also remember you were head and shoulders taller than everyone else, and the friends who were guarding and hiding you—couldn't hide you. (I had this feeling that I actually saw your soul in the dream. You were in a white, flowing, loose, luxurious dress, a continuation of your body—and your soul.) My memory of you in this dream is like algae in water, with all its movement. You were quietly being rocked by some sea, separating me from you—nothing happened, but I knew one thing—I loved you with such fervor (a silent frenzy), I wanted you to the point of self-annihilation, so that I feel completely emptied (and overwhelmed) now.

Where do I go with all this? To you, for I will never believe that dreams make mistakes, that a dream can be wrong, that I can be mistaken in a dream. (Everywhere else—but.) This is what I wrote, before I had the dream, it's my guarantee: my favorite form of communication is sleep. Sleep is for me complete freedom (inescapable), the air I need to breathe. My weather, my light, my hour of the day, my season, my latitude and my longitude. Only in the dream am I—myself. The rest is random.

Opening the World of Sapphic Feelings

By Olgerta Kharitonova

For us, Russian lesbians, Marina Tsvetaeva's texts became pathways to a protected forest, where feelings, relationships, words, meanings, values grew—and these texts felt very close, quite understandable and dear to us to the point of heartache, but they were unknown and banned in official Russian culture. Marina Tsvetaeva not only opened the world of sapphic feelings to us, but also gave us a language for expressing a passion—for the manifestation of that love that blazed in our souls despite the imposed standards of Soviet life.

I was born on Stalin Street in 1959. Stalin himself had died six years earlier, but his monuments were not yet dismantled and streets were not renamed. Can you imagine a similar situation in 1951 in Germany where someone would be living on Hitler Street? Although the cult of Stalin had been exposed by 1956 in the Soviet Union, the ideology remained. This curtain of silence over aspects of life, phenomena, ideas that did not fit into the Procrustean bed of a beautiful communist future ideal was the main strategy for spreading socialist ideology.

The loudest silence surrounded human sexuality. As was declared during perestroika and glasnost, "we don't have sex"—these were the words of one participant in the Leningrad-Boston teleconference ("Women Speak to Women"), which aired on July 17, 1986. The sentence was taken out of context and given a distorted meaning, but it became a catchphrase because it accurately reflected the bitter irony of attitudes towards the entire sexual sphere in the Soviet Union. We were not told either at school or at home where babies came from. We learned about this in the schoolyard from our girlfriends. I was about seven years old when one girl told me that a man's "thing" looked like a snail, and I mentally tried to envision a huge snail fitting into a man's underwear, twisting into a Fibonacci spiral—I couldn't imagine it, the picture did not come together, and in the end I got tired of it all and gave up my useless attempts. When I was about eight, I heard from another girl about how intercourse between a man and a woman occurred—the picture was extremely unsightly, and I kept turning it over in my head with a feeling of disgust for a long time. I even learned about menstruation from girls at the pioneer camp: why were women subjected to such terrible physical punishment. So the blood on my underwear I perceived to be associated with something shameful, dirty, and sick.

We didn't talk about human reproduction in anatomy lessons at school. There were pictures of an egg and a sperm in the biology textbook, but how the sperm got into the same space as the egg was not explained. The further development of a fetus was covered in great detail. The scientific side of the subject was taught well in Soviet schools.

The appearance of a woman in a slip or a bra in Soviet films was next to impossible: many such scenes were banned. And this was quite normal, since any form of human sexuality was banned in the USSR. While films about love were released, we received a minimal idea of romantic relationships between a man and a woman. Only romantic or family ones, of course! And only between a man and a woman—there was no other way!

Nevertheless, sincere warm relationships with girlfriends were viewed as legitimate female friendships. Such relationships were formed between classmates or in pioneer camps, where our parents sent us for the summer. Now, when I remember these friendships, I realize there was a lot of love in them: we would try to win the attention of a girl we liked, to become closer to her, to start a correspondence with her so that we could exchange letters, then we'd start going everywhere together, guarding her from other possible friendships—it was very much like a romantic relationship with a boy, only without kisses. Often, in such friendships, girls became so much closer to each other than when falling in love with a boy. They would look at a boy from afar as an object, an object of love, they would idealize him; they were shy to approach him. A girlfriend was perceived as the beloved.

When I was 16, I came across a book by Sigmund Freud about Leonardo da Vinci's homosexuality. I had no idea who Freud was at the time, but I was interested in Leonardo the artist. I read the entire essay in one sitting. It was published in the USSR in the 1920s, before psychoanalysis was banned. That was how I learned the word "homosexuality" and I was horrified. Being young at the time, the dream that Freud analyzed disgusted me—I didn't think that books were written on "such things," or that "such things" were characteristic of a great artist. In Leonardo da Vinci's dream, a large bird stuck its tail into the artist's mouth. Freud interpreted the bird's tail as a phallus and derived from this Leonardo's desire for oral sex with a man. What a nightmare, and disgusting, and loathsome—these were the feelings that overwhelmed me, knowing practically nothing about sex, much less about male-to-male sex. But that very same feeling of disgust held a fear that I myself was "tainted" by homosexuality. At that time, I was experiencing a strong crush on a teacher. After young girl friendships, this was the next step towards a full-fledged same-sex relationship. My crush remained purely romantic, platonic, without anything physiological, and without any desire for sexual intimacy.

Thus, my first encounter with "homosexuality"—as homosexuality was called in the Soviet Union—was, to say the least, unpleasant: it brought up revulsion, repudiation, and categorical rejection. In my heart, I was shutting the door on such thoughts forever.

Two years passed, I graduated from school, entered a technical school, left my hometown, moved into a dormitory . . . and fell in love. This time, everything seemed serious. I was already 18 years old, and the girl I liked was my age, a classmate. We tried to spend all our time together both during classes at the technical school and after school: we walked, went to the movies, and since we studied in the architecture department, we did our drawings and planned projects together. At first, we simply enjoyed being together, talking, getting to know each other's tastes and interests. A few months after we began getting closer, we moved on to kissing. Tatyana was very beautiful and I had long wanted to casually touch her, to caress her, to hug her and, of course, to kiss her. But I was timid—such emotional trepidation was unknown to me until then. I had been in love with girls before, but physical attraction had not been awakened. This time, in addition to emotional, I wanted physical intimacy. I was the initiator. I saw that Tatyana liked me too, that she was interested in me, but at the same time she told me how much she liked the actor who played Romeo in Zeffirelli's film. The thought of falling in love with Juliet, and not Romeo, never came to her mind. That thought had not come to my mind, either; I did not think about my feelings, I simply felt a desire for physical intimacy. And it happened: very quietly, gradually, embarrassed by our nakedness before the gaze of the other, we learned how to love one another. We learned how to respond with our bodies. We didn't know anything about erogenous zones, the clitoris, orgasms. We knew nothing, we didn't say anything, because words meant nothing—they were just sounds, behind which there was emptiness. We were Eve and Lilith in the Garden of Eden.

We also knew no shame when we experienced intimacy. Shame came from the outside world, which intruded into our relationship. We erected thick stone walls around ourselves—a tower made of black marble. While studying architecture, we built everything according to building codes and regulations. We remained shy and sensitive lovers, bosom friends, shameless lovers, discoverers of each other's worlds and creators of our universe in our dorm. In the outside world, we were classmates and girlfriends, just friends, because female friendship was such an ordinary thing that it did not arouse suspicion.

In my hometown I had a friend with whom I shared a desk all my school years. When I moved to another region to study at the technical school, we started corresponding, telling each other about our changed lives. At that time, she also fell in love, though with a young man. I still have this correspondence, where she writes about her feelings and I about mine. Since we had known each other since childhood, we understood each other perfectly and we were not embarrassed by the fact that she was writing about a young man and I about a girl—our experience of feelings was the same. And our feelings turned out to be identical, the gender of the partner did not play a part. We were equally happy in some moments or unhappy in others, we rejoiced at the same things and were upset about similar things. Love knew no gender differences, if it was love.

I first heard the word "lesbian" in 1982, when I entered the philosophy department of Moscow State University. More progressive young people came together there, with greater knowledge, intelligence, resulting in critical minds, able to see the seamy side of everyday life and, if necessary, they could even discern corruption in semolina porridge. As soon as I entered, during entrance exams, my future classmates were calling two young students "lesbians." They were from the same city and always went out together. It turned out later they had hurried off to Moscow to find men to marry. They had that one goal and there had been no intimacy between them. Nevertheless, for me, I learned the word "lesbian" was the association that arose in any observer's mind, and I realized that we—Tatyana, my first true love, and I—were lesbians, and not the two young women who went to conquer the capital. That was how I got acquainted with the term describing myself. And I liked it, and not the word "homosexuality."

The library at Moscow State University was very good, especially in our building, where the history and philology departments were also located. I quickly found out where the island of Lesbos was, who Sappho was, and even read some of her poems translated by Vikenty Veresaev. That was how my acquaintance with lesbian culture began, or, as I later heard another name for it, "culture with a Sapphic touch." In the same library, I accidentally came across Marina Tsvetaeva's *Story of Sonechka* in hand-bound sheets from a thick literary magazine called *Novy Mir.* The first part of the novella was published in 1976, and the second part of Tsvetaeva's text in 1979.

I played out *Story of Sonechka* completely and perfectly. It was I who waited for Sonechka, it was I who lived Sonechka, it was I who breathed her. I didn't really understand then who Marina Tsvetaeva was, but while I was reading the story, I was her. I had the same feelings for Sonechka. And like Tsvetaeva, I didn't call them lesbian. It had become clear to me even earlier that there was no a word for it in the beginning. There was a feeling, and only later was a name invented for it. Just as I loved my Tatyana, not knowing the word "lesbian," so Marina Tsvetaeva loved Sonechka Holliday, without hanging labels on her feelings that could have been disapproved by society. And not because she was afraid of society's reaction—I don't know a woman more fearless in her feelings—but simply because a word sets boundaries: we use this term to denote this phenomenon, and everything else does not fall under this definition. Tsvetaeva could not live within boundaries: all her feelings were limitless. However, I felt the sapphic touch in *Story of Sonechka* right away—my tuning fork was already tuned to this very pitch.

I came across Marina Tsvetaeva's poems later. They were not published in the Soviet Union for a long time. Only after Stalin's death, having returned to Moscow from Siberian exile, where she had been sent in the late thirties, Tsvetaeva's daughter, Ariadna Efron, began to push for the publication of her mother's works. This process turned out to be complex and difficult to resolve; it met with desperate resistance from the Writers' Union. After all, Tsvetaeva emigrated after the revolution, meaning she was a traitor to the motherland. Her poems were "ideologically harmful" for Soviet people. The first collection of her work, *Selected Works*, was published only in 1961 and quickly became a rarity. The real discovery of Marina Tsvetaeva's work occurred in the eighties and nineties of the last century, during *perestroika* and after the collapse of the USSR, when the dictatorship of the Communist Party became a thing of the past.

At that time, a lot was revealed to us. The thing is that when you live in an information vacuum, when you see only happy or unhappy people around you, people in love or breaking up, married or divorced, couples consisting of a man and a woman—of course, a man and a woman—then you involuntarily begin to think that you are "the only one," the only lesbian in the Soviet Union. And then it suddenly turned out that this was not so, that there were other women in our country, in love, erotically-oriented, emotionally attached not to a man, but to a woman. The feeling of utter loneliness began to disintegrate not so much because of meeting real lesbians (I hadn't had that experience for long), but because of the literary evidence of their existence (in books). Lesbians began to be discussed publicly, their works began to be published. Two or three films about lesbian relationships were shown on TV (foreign films, of course, shown late at night). Information leaked out sparingly, quietly, half-hidden, veiled. The crack in this secret had barely opened. And yet the process had begun.

The play *Marina*, brought to our province from Moscow, made a strong impression on me. I happened to see a poster on the street, read the cast of characters and realized that this play was about the relationship between Marina Tsvetaeva and Sofia Parnok. I had already heard something about this relationship, but very sparingly and through rumors. And suddenly there was an entire production only about them. I saw the play three times—all three evenings that it played in our city. If, in *Story of Sonechka* the sapphic touch was like a shepherd's bell, then in this performance it thundered like an alarm. The performance was based on Marina Tsvetaeva's Girlfriend cycle of poems. At that time, I knew only one poem from the cycle: "Cuddling under my plush comforter." A song to this text was in a film watched by millions of Soviet moviegoers, and none of them knew that the poem was about the relationship between two women, and not a man and a woman as shown in the film.

I was able to read the entire cycle two years later when the seven volumes of Marina Tsvetaeva's *Collected Work* were published. Since the late eighties, many have published selected poems by Tsvetaeva, but the *Girlfriend* cycle only appeared in the first volume of this 1994 edition. I was lucky to get the book as soon as it was released. So I recognized in the poems those lines that I'd previously heard from the stage in the play *Marina.* From the poems of the *Girlfriend* cycle, you can understand and feel the relationship that connected Tsvetaeva and Parnok—the poems have everything, and what was not there, wasn't in the poems. There are an infinite number of interpretations in the abyss of speculation. But the essence is simple—the love between two women. Everything else is unimportant, the details are simply vignettes.

The couple, Marina Tsvetaeva and Sofia Parnok, became icons for Russian lesbians. Probably, in many countries there are such women—symbols. They validate lesbian identity, and people dedicate their books to them. Lesbian culture grew on their foundation. We were lucky in Russia, we started with high-quality written works: the poems of Sofia Parnok, who was an open lesbian in the Silver Age of Russian culture, and the works of Marina Tsvetaeva, who did not want to consider herself a lesbian, but whose sapphic tone in poetry sounded throughout the world. Moscow lesbians as well as those coming to the capital from the provinces would go to the Tsvetaeva Museum on Boris and Gleb Lane as if they were going to a lesbian mecca. At the grave of Sofia Parnok at the Vvedenskoye Cemetery, they would leave not only flowers, but also notes to each other, addressing unknown women in hopes of finding a kindred spirit. At the Pere Lachaise Cemetery in Paris, on the grave of Oscar Wilde, gays left kisses and lipstick marks (now the monument is surrounded by transparent panels). For Russian lesbians, the stone cross on Parnok's grave has become an iconic landmark.

In Russian society, lesbians are not recognized as people, our rights are limited and we are locked in silence. There is still a conspiracy of silence around us. A girl or young woman who feels her otherness cannot open up—she has no one to talk to about it. In Russia, even the Internet is restricted now. But these two pillars stand: Tsvetaeva and Parnok—they have given us support and hope. The hope that girls in Russia will grow up and choose the path that is rightfully theirs. There is not only one scenario, there are many, despite the fact that Russian society is trying to narrow the horizon of possibilities down to the traditional family. However, if a young woman picks up a volume of Tsvetaeva, opens it to the pages of *Story of Sonechka*, she'll get choked up with tenderness . . .

Olgerta Kharitonova,
feminist philosopher, creator of the lesbian samizdat journal *Ostrov* [Island]

Olgerta Kharitonova is a feminist philosopher and member of the LGBT rights movement in Russia.

She was born in 1959 in the Urals in the USSR, studied at the Philosophy Department of Moscow State University and defended her dissertation on the philosophy of death in 1995 at the Ural State University.

In 1998, she moved to Moscow and joined the lesbian life there. She began to publish a magazine for lesbians called *Ostrov* [Island], which continued the tradition of Soviet samizdat. The first issue of *Ostrov* was published in December 1999. In addition to the magazine itself, literary supplements were published. The last issue, No. 61, was published in December 2014, after fifteen years of the project's existence.

Due to the military aggression of the Russian Federation against Ukraine, Olgerta moved to Germany in 2015, where she now lives with her wife. During Putin's rule, the LGBT movement for openness in Russia has been strongly suppressed. The

LGBT community in the Russian Federation was declared extremist by the government, and many participants have been subject to criminal prosecution.

Olgerta wrote and released her *Manifesto of the Feminist Movement of Russia* in 2014, and since then she has focused her attention on developing feminist theory: writing books, articles, and other texts.

Selected Books by and about Tsvetaeva

Much of Marina Tsvetaeva's work is available in English and Russian on the internet now. My translations into English of the complete *Girlfriend Poems* and *Story of Sonechka* in this book are among the first and are not available on the Internet. My translation of *Letter to an Amazon*, the first in English, was published in 1994 in an early issue of the *Harvard Gay and Lesbian Review*.

Efron, Ariadna. *No Love Without Poetry: The Memoirs of Marina Tsvetaeva's Daughter.* Translated by Diane Nemec Ignashev. Northwestern University Press, 1989.

Fieler, Lily. *Marina Tsvetaeva: The Double Beat of Heaven and Hell.* Duke University Press, 1994.

Franeta, Sonja. *My Pink Road to Russia: Tales of Amazons, Peasants, and Queers.* Dacha Books, 2015. (I have chapters in my book on Tsvetaeva and on Parnok).

Franeta, Sonja. *Pink Flamingos: 10 Siberian Interviews.* Dacha Books, 2017.

Karlinsky, Simon. *Marina Tsvetaeva: The Woman, her World, and her Poetry.* Cambridge University Press, 1985.

Kossman, Nina. *Other Shepherds: Poems with Translations from Marina Tsvetaeva.* Poets & Traitors Press, 2020. (A mix of Kossman's poetry and her translations of Tsvetaeva).

Polyakova, Sofia. Закатные Оны Дни: Цветаева и Парнок[*The Sunset Days of Yore: Tsvetaeva and Parnok*]. Ardis, 1983.

Schmidt, Paul, trans. *The Stray Dog Cabaret: A Book of Russian Poems.* New York Review of Books, 2007.

Tsvetaeva, Marina. *A Captive Spirit: Selected Prose.* Edited and translated by J. Marin King. Ardis, 1980–2004.

Tsvetaeva, Marina. *Art in the Light of Conscience: Eight Essays on Poetry.* Translated by Angela Livingstone. Harvard University Press, 1992.

Tsvetaeva, Marina. *Bride of Ice: New and Selected Poems of Marina Tsvetaeva.* Translated by Elaine Feinstein. Carcanet, 2011.

Tsvetaeva, Marina. *Dark Elderberry Branch: Poems of Marina Tsvetaeva.* Translated by Ilya Kaminsky and Jean Valentine. Alice James Books, 2012. (Wonderful translations by two wonderful poets)

Tsvetaeva, Marina. *Histoire de Sonetchka.* Translated by Veronique Lossky. Clemence Hiver Editeur, 1991.

Tsvetaeva, Marina. *Letter to an Amazon.* Translated by Sonja Franeta. First published in *The Gay and Lesbian Review Worldwide*, formerly: *The Harvard Gay and Lesbian Review* (1994-1999).

Tsvetaeva, Marina. *Mon frere feminin, Lettre a l' Amazon.* Mercure de France, 1979.

Tsvetaeva, Marina. *Selected Poems.* Translated by Elaine Feinstin. Penguin, 1971.

Tsvietaieva, Marina. *Mi Hermano Feminino: Carta a la Amazona.* Translated by Josa Fructuosa. Flores, 2018. (Spanish edition of *Letter to an Amazon.*)

Sofia Parnok Recommendation:

Burgin, Diana. *Sophia Parnok: the Life and Work of Russia's Sappho.* New York University Press, 1994.

Name Glossary

Vladimir Alexeyev (Volodya, Volodechka) (1883-1922) Actor in the Third Studio. Tsvetaeva said with him she could share "the masculine in me."

Pavel Antokolsky (Pavlik) (1896-1978) Actor in the Third Studio of the Moscow Art Theater, later director in the Vakhtangov Theater. He was a poet who published a book in 1922. He wrote a memoir about Tsvetaeva and her theater work. After reading one of his poems, Tsvetaeva looked him up and then became involved in the Third Studio.

Yuri Alexandrovich Zavadsky (Yura) (1894-1972) Actor in the Third Studio, who later became a famous actor and director. He eventually moved to the Stanislavsky Theater. His sister Vera also had a career in the theater. Yuri and Antokolsky were lovers when Tsvetaeva met them.

Sofia Evgenievna Holliday (Sonechka, Sonya) (1896-1935) Her last name is written and pronounced as Gollidey in Russian. Her father was English and her mother was Russian. An actress in the Third Studio, she and Tsvetaeva met in the Moscow Art Theater and had an erotic relationship. *Story of Sonechka* is Tsvetaeva's portrait of the one "she loved more than anyone."

Evgeny Bagrationovich Vakhtangov (Evgeny Bagrationych) (1883-1922) Director and founder of several studios of the Moscow Art Theater. After his death, the Third Studio became the Vakhtangov Theater. He was famous for his innovative and expressionist style.

Vakhtang Levanovich Mchedelov (1884-1924) Actor, teacher, and director at the Second Studio.

Alexey Alexandrovich Stakhovich (1856-1919) Actor and part of the Moscow Art Theater. Formerly part of the Russian Imperial Guard, he taught actors deportment and etiquette. His suicide had a big effect on Tsvetaeva.

Ariadna Efron (Alya, Alechka) (1912-1975) Artist and writer. The oldest daughter of Marina Tsvetaeva and Sergey Efron. She is a child in *Story of Sonechka*. She went into exile with her mother in Europe but then returned to Soviet Russia. Arrested in 1939 for espionage, she was sentenced to the gulag again. After her release in 1955, she spent her life collecting and publishing her mother's work. Her memoir is *No Love Without Poetry: Memoirs of Marina Tsvetaeva's Daughter.*

Acknowledgements

Decades after Marina's death, in St. Petersburg, then Leningrad USSR, another Sonya—Soviet scholar Sofia Polyakova—had been combing bookshops for traces of Marina Tsvetaeva and Sofia Parnok. Polyakova gave us a very important book—a revelation to the world of their lesbian/sapphic relationship. Her book, called *Sunset Days of Yore: Tsvetaeva and Parnok* (Ardis, 1983), published the entire *Girlfriend* cycle of poems along with a commentary about the women's lives and relationship, as well as other relevant poems by them. It documented their sapphic poetry, their daily lives, their social surroundings, and literary and romantic connections. Published by Ardis Press in Michigan, it was with the help of Russian gay scholar Simon Karlinsky, a Tsvetaeva specialist, who helped smuggle the book into the U.S. Polyakova was also the first to publish Sofia Parnok's *Collected Works* in Russian.

In 1993, a year before she died, I had the privilege of meeting and interviewing Sofia Polyakova. She spoke to me about her research on both Tsvetaeva and Parnok and showered me with stories and photographs. Having tea with her and her partner was a special treat. They appreciated the fact that I was a lesbian and we managed to do some flirting—but I was also a Sonja and there was that fortuitous connection through the name Sofia—me, Polyakova, and the Sofias in Tsvetaeva's life.

It was 1993, beginning of *perestroika*, the period following the breakup of the repressive Soviet Union. I got a taste of life in the privacy of lesbian homes from this older couple. Unfortunately, Sofia Polyakova died the following year. What an amazing accomplishment—to make public the real Marina Tsvetaeva!

Needless to say, when Polyakova's research was made available, Marina became an icon for lesbians, bisexuals and queers throughout the Soviet Union.

Befriending Simon, who was my former professor at U.C. Berkeley, was another inspiration for this work. Sometime before my 1991 trip to Russia for the first gay and Lesbian Symposium and Film Festival, he alerted me to this groundbreaking book. I began to learn more and more about the lesbian side of Marina Tsvetaeva. His book *Marina Tsvetaeva: the Woman, Her World, and Her Poetry* has been invaluable to me. Not only was it a great source of facts about Marina but it was so accessible and beautifully written. I have always admired Simon for his excellent work revealing the hidden history of queer literature and art in Russia.

I would like to acknowledge the help and support of my dear friend Elena Gusyatinskaya, leader of the Moscow LGBT Archives, who consulted with me on my translation work. We have worked together since we met following the 1991 Symposium and Film Festival in Moscow. As a French translator, Elena gave invaluable assistance with the translation of *Letter to an Amazon*, which was written in French originally. Veronika Losskaya's French translation of *Story of Sonechka* was beautiful and while my knowledge of French was not fluent, it was still an excellent reference for me.

My greatest inspiration to produce this book, as well as my other two books, has come from the queer community in the former Soviet Republics. I have made many friends and met so many wonderful people during the conference and later in the 1990s when I traveled and worked in Moscow, St. Petersburg, Siberia, and Ukraine.

So many friends and co-writers have encouraged me in this endeavor, there are too many to name. I appreciate all of their love and encouragement over the years.

Three earlier translations of the Girlfriend poems were published in *River Styx*, number 37, 1983. I am grateful to the editors and readers there.

Above all, I want to thank Julie Enszer and *Sinister Wisdom* for their enthusiasm and support in publishing Marina's work in my translation. This is a dream come true for me.

Translator Biography

Sonja Franeta is a translator, writer, educator, and activist born in the Bronx to an immigrant Yugoslav family. She received a BA from New York University in 1973, majoring in English and Russian. After receiving an MA in Russian literature from New York University, she earned another Master's in Comparative Literature in 1976 from the University of California at Berkeley.

Her interest in Russia crystallized when she joined the first queer delegation to Russia in 1991, organized by IGLHRC. Sonja continued to be in Russia during the 1990s in its transformative period. She taught English in Moscow, managed a project for wheelchair activists in Central Siberia, and organized a queer film festival in Tomsk. Her translations and articles about Russian queers, her poems and stories have appeared in the U.S. and internationally.

In 2004, she published *Rozovye Flamingo* (*Pink Flamingos: 10 Siberian Interviews,* in Russian), in collaboration with friends at the LGBT Archives in Moscow. She returned to teaching (English and ESL) in the San Francisco area, all the while translating both literary and technical texts. In 2015, Sonja published her memoir *My Pink Road to Russia: Tales of Amazons, Peasants and Queers*, now translated into Russian. In 2017, she translated into English and self-published *Pink Flamingos.* Other interviews are available in the Pink Flamingo Archives. She continues to read and translate other Russian favorites, especially poet Marina Tsvetaeva.

She and her spouse, Sue, have lived part of the time in St. Petersburg, Florida and in lovely Laredo on the north coast of Spain. She has always loved books and continues reading them and making them. Writing and translating are her passions.

Endnotes

Notes:

Part One: Pavlik and Yuri

[I] Alexander Pushkin (1799–1837) Russia's most popular poet, called the father of Russian literature. The Decembrists were a group of radicals who tried to prevent the Tsar from taking the throne in 1825; the Preobrazhensky Regiment guarded the Tsar. Pushkin sided with the Decembrists.

[II] Studio Three was part of the Moscow Art Theater. This is the group Tsvetaeva worked with in 1919 and where she met Sonechka and the others.

[III] This line is from a poem by French poet Victor Hugo and begins *Story of Sonechka.*

[IV] Edmond About wrote this book in the mid-19th century before Sonechka was born. A Tsvetaeva mystification—he was not of course writing about Sonechka.

[V] "White Nights" was a short story written in 1848 by Dostoevsky adapted for the stage by the Moscow Art Theater.

[VI] *The Miracle of St. Anthony* by Maeterlink was a play staged by the Moscow Art Theater. Yuri Zavadsky played the main role of St. Anthony.

[VII] Natasha Rostova is one of the main characters of Tolstoy's *War and Peace*; the others named are female literary characters and the young man Mignon, Goethe's poetic character.

[VIII] Sonechka's father's name was Evgeny, so her patronymic (middle name) was Evgenievna. Sonechka's patronymic connects her with Evgeny Vakhtangov, one of the theater directors.

[IX] Alexey Alexandrovich Stakhovich (1856-1919) was an actor and part of the Moscow Art Theater. This is the third of three poems dedicated to Stakhovich. The second one is below.

[X] *The Green Ring* is a play by queer poet Zinaida Gippius (1869-1945).

[XI] Francois Bonivard was a Genevan patriot imprisoned and immortalized by poet Lord Byron in his poem "Prisoner of Chillon."

[XII] Yuri Slezkin (1885-1947) a playwright of the times, his last name means tears in Russian.

[XIII] Konstantin Stanislavsky (1863-1938), a dramatic innovator and a founder of the Moscow Art Theater. His system and books became foundational to actor training internationally.

[XIV] Vladimir Khodasevich (1886-1936) a poet at literary critic who was always favorable to the writings of Tsvetaeva.

[XV] Tsvetaeva is referring to the Spanish Civil War (1936-1939). She was writing this in 1937.

[XVI] In 1918, Novocherkassk was an important battle site between the Red (Bolshevik) forces and the White (anti-Bolshevik) forces. The next year the White Guard was pushed back in many different places throughout the country and finally defeated in 1920.

[XVII] Kolchak (1874-1920) Admiral of the Black Sea fleet and head of the White Guard offensive.

Notes:

Part Two: Volodya

[I] French poet Victor Hugo's famous poem "Ce siecle avait deux ans" is about Napoleon becoming Emperor and includes Hugo's own birth in 1802. This couplet is from the poem.

[II] The Russian Revolution began in 1917 and it took some years for the transformation to take place. After much struggle, the Soviet Union was founded in 1922. Women's liberation was a part of the Revolution.

[III] Red Youth were the young communists, later called Pioneers. They sheltered in the theater to rest from the fighting. Tsvetaeva did not support the revolutionaries at the time.

[IV] In Russia, people are given a first name and a patronymic, which their father's name plus a suffix. Marina Ivanovna Tsvetaeva means her father's name was Ivan.

[V] Alexander Blok wrote this poem in 1913 dedicated to the great poet Anna Akhmatova, when she was young.

[VI] Prince S M. Volkonsky (1860-1937) an aristocrat, director of the imperial theaters. Tsvetaeva admired him and wrote poetry about him.

[VII] Alexander Scriabin (1872-1915) the composer.

[VIII] This and the next two excerpts are from Marina Tsvetaeva's poem "The Comedian" (1919) about a comedian who makes others laugh while inside he feels alone.

[IX] Bettina Brentano, a writer, had an epistolary relationship with Goethe. Fackelzug is a torchlight procession of honor.

[X] In Russian folktales, Baba Yaga was the female equivalent of the bogeyman, the wicked witch. Not simply evil or good, she could be wise and helpful.

[XI] "Ruslan and Lyudmila" (1820) Pushkin's first long poem; it made him famous overnight.

[XII] *Death and the Maiden* was a famous song and string quartet piece by Franz Schubert.

[XIII] Pushkin wrote a play called *The Feast During the Plague* (1830).

[XIV] Pechorin, the main character of Lermontov's Russian classic *A Hero of Our Time* (1840).

[XV] Allusion to a famous poem "The Dream" by Lermontov (1841) about a soldier dying alone and his bond with a woman who is far away.

[XVI] Sonechka embarks on a list of popular poetry she likes, from this anthology of the times.

[XVII] *Sixty Years of Memories* by Ernest Legouvè—a memoir of prominent French 19th century figures published in the 1880s. A section of the book was devoted to Maria Malbran (La Malibran) who was a celebrated opera singer. She died at 28.

[XVIII] Cosette and Jean Valjean—main characters of Victor Hugo's novel *Les Miserables* (1862).

[XIX] Nastenka is the heroine of "White Nights."

[XX] Alexander Kolchak (1874-1920) one of the main commanders of the White Army (anti-Bolshevik) during the Russian Revolution.

[XXI] Dostoevsky's novel about an adolescent lesbian crush that is eventually recipricated. The novel was never finished because Dostoevsky was sent to Siberia.

Notes:

Part Three: Sonechka's Departure

[I] Old Style refers to the old Julian calendar, thirteen days behind the European Gregorian Calendar. Russia made the shift to the Gregorian in 1918.

[II] *The Magic Lantern* (1912) was Marina Tsvetaeva's excellent debut, her first published book of poetry. She was only 18.

[III] A typical Russian custom—to sit together before a departure in silence and pray for safety.

[IV] Greetings over the threshold are considered a bad omen in Russia.

[V] The *Adventures* was a poetic play about love by Tsvetaeva.

[VI] Nikolaus Lenau, an Austrian lyric poet (1802-1850).

[VII] Irina, the second daughter of Marina Tsvetaeva, born in 1917, died of hunger in February of 1920 in a state children's home in Kuntsevo, near Moscow.

Notes:

The Girlfriend Poems

[I] Fifteen poems form the traditional cycle of Tsvetaeva's love poems, translated as *The Girlfriend Poems.* The word girlfriend in Russian [*podruga*] can also mean woman friend or woman lover, whereas in English, girlfriend is more commonly used to describe a lesbian lover.

[II] Bolshaya Lubyanka is a major street in the center of Moscow.

[III] Tsvetaeva is referring to Sofia Parnok's reddish brown hair.

[IV] Tsvetaeva may be thinking of herself as Electra to Parnok's Orestes. Major figures in Greek mythology, they were siblings and very devoted to each other.

[V] The Spartan boy suffered great pain rather than admit guilt. Tsvetaeva, too, could be secretive and could endure pain.

Notes:

Restored Poems by Tsvetaeva to Parnok

[I] Additional poems, collected by Sofia Polyakova in her book, only available in Russian. According to Polyakova, the additional poems by Tsvetaeva, although omitted or not included in the *Girlfriend* cycle, reflect her time with Parnok (1914-1916).

Notes:

Letter to an Amazon

[I] This first translation in English, edited for this book, of Tsvetaeva's *Lettre a l'Amazone* is from the French original. I was assisted by my dear friend Elena Gusyatinskaya, a French translator. The version we used was a small blue book, published under the title *Mon frère féminin* (my female brother), with no date. We know it was published only after Tsvetaeva's death. Tsvetaeva, Marina, "Letter to an Amazon," translated by Sonja Franeta (October 31, 1994). *The Harvard Gay & Lesbian Review.* **1** (4): 9 (now *The Gay and Lesbian Review Worldwide*).

[II] In Greek mythology, Orpheus was torn apart by the Maenads and his severed head washed ashore on the island of Lesbos.

[III] This great poet was Sappho and her Island of birth was Lesbos.

[IV] In Russian the adjective for straight or heterosexual women is "normal." While this is not used in French, Tsvetaeva may have used the Russian here.

Notes:

Letter to Salomea Halpern

[I] Salomea Halpern, formerly a Georgian princess, was one of Tsvetaeva's benefactresses in Paris. They also had an extensive letter exchange over the years. Written at the time of her work on *Letter to an Amazon,* this letter captures her strong attraction to Salomea.

Other Books from *Sinister Wisdom*

SWANA Dykes, edited by Khadijah Pitts-Ceesay and Nikki Luna, 2026

*The Complete Works of Pat Parker (*10th Anniversary Edition), edited by Julie R. Enszer, 2026

The Dyke and the Dybbuk, Ellen Galford, 2026

Acts of Resistance, Cheryl Clarke, 2026

Essential Poems by Pat Parker, edited by SaraEllen Strongman, 2025

Black Lesbian in White America and Other Writings, Anita Cornwell, edited by Briona Simone Jones, 2025

Melting in Your Mouth: The Early Work of Chocolate Waters, Chocolate Waters, 2025

S/HE, Minne Bruce Pratt, 2024

Blue Heat: A Portfolio of Poems and Drawings, Alexis De Veaux, 2024

Hungerheart: The Story of a Soul, C. Marshall St. John, 2025

The Pagoda: A Lesbian Community By the Sea, Rose Norman, 2024

The Highest Apple: Sappho and the Lesbian Poetic Tradition, Judy Grahn, 2023

Fire-Rimmed Eden: Selected Poems, Lynn Lonidier, 2023

A Sturdy Yes of a People: Selected Writings, Joan Nestle, 2022

Para las Duras: Una Fenomonologia Lesbiana / For the Hard Ones: A Lesbian Phenomenology, tatiana de la tierra, 2018

Sister Love: The Letters of Audre Lorde and Pat Parker 1974-1989, edited by Julie R. Enszer, 2018

What Can I Ask: New and Selected Poems 1975-2014, Elana Dykewomon, 2015

Living as a Lesbian, Cheryl Clarke, 2014

Crime Against Nature, Minne Bruce Pratt, 2013

Sinister Wisdom is a multicultural lesbian literary & art journal founded in 1976. *Sinister Wisdom* works to create multi-class, multicultural, multi-gender, multi-racial, world-wide intergenerational queer and lesbian spaces. Through publishing quarterly issues, a Sapphic Classics book series, and offering educational programs, Sinister Wisdom nurtures lesbian communities. *Sinister Wisdom* is a living archive that celebrates the multiplicity of lesbian identities across races, classes, genders, abilities, and lived experiences. *Sinister Wisdom* recognizes the power of language and art to create radical, empowering, resilient, and joyous sanctuaries that build and sustain vibrant lesbian futures.

Former editors and publishers:
Harriet Ellenberger (aka Desmoines)
and Catherine Nicholson (1976-1981)
Michelle Cliff and Adrienne Rich (1981-1983)
Michaele Uccella (1983-1984)
Melanie Kaye/Kantrowitz (1983-1987)
Elana Dykewomon (1987-1994)
Caryatis Cardea (1991-1994)
Akiba Onada-Sikwoia (1995-1997)
Margo Mercedes Rivera-Weiss (1997-2000)
Fran Day (2004-2010)
Julie R. Enszer & Merry Gangemi (2010-2013)
Julie R. Enszer (2013-)

Sinister Wisdom is a US non-profit organization; donations to support the work and distribution of *Sinister Wisdom* are welcome and appreciated, including legacy gifts in wills and trusts.

www.ingramcontent.com/pod-product-compliance
Lightning Source LLC
LaVergne TN
LVHW090022210826
846010LV00030B/228
9781970841022